1 and 2 Thessalonians

The Contextual Critical Commentary

The Contextual Critical Commentary (CCC) on the Bible offers students, scholars, and clergy an affordable and scholarly resource to inform the reading and interpretation of the books of the Bible. The CCC integrates contextual work that critically explores the historical, literary, and theological context of biblical books in relation to the ancient Near Eastern and Greco-Roman worlds of ancient Israel, Judah, and the early church. The historical context will provide a background for future contextual readings of these texts, their reception, and their interpretation within Judaism and Christianity. Finally, the ancient context and key turning points in reception history will inform the concerns of contemporary readings of biblical texts, suggesting ways that their past contexts can guide both scholarly readers and readers in faith communities today.

1 and 2 Thessalonians

A. Andrew Das

CASCADE *Books* • Eugene, Oregon

FIRST AND SECOND THESSALONIANS
The Contextual Critical Commentary

Copyright © 2026 A. Andrew Das. All rights reserved. Except for brief quotations in critical publications or reviews, no part of this book may be reproduced in any manner without prior written permission from the publisher. Write: Permissions, Wipf and Stock Publishers, 199 W. 8th Ave., Suite 3, Eugene, OR 97401.

Cascade Books
An Imprint of Wipf and Stock Publishers
199 W. 8th Ave., Suite 3
Eugene, OR 97401

www.wipfandstock.com

PAPERBACK ISBN: 978-1-6667-6623-3
HARDCOVER ISBN: 978-1-6667-6624-0
EBOOK ISBN: 978-1-6667-6625-7

Cataloging-in-Publication data:

Names: Das, A. Andrew, author.

Title: First and Second Thessalonians / A. Andrew Das.

Description: Eugene, OR: Cascade Books, 2026. | The Contextual Critical Commentary. | Includes bibliographical references.

Identifiers: ISBN: 978-1-6667-6623-3 (paperback). | ISBN: 978-1-6667-6624-0 (hardcover). | ISBN: 978-1-6667-6625-7 (ebook).

Subjects: LCSH: Bible.—Thessalonians—Commentaries.

Classification: BS2775.53 D37 2026 (print). | BS2775.53 (epub).

VERSION NUMBER 01/26/26

Unless otherwise stated, Scripture translations are the author's own.

Scripture quotations marked NETS are from A New English Translation of the Septuagint, ©2007 by the International Organization for Septuagint and Cognate Studies, Inc. Used by permission of Oxford University Press. All rights reserved.

Contents

Introduction | vii
Abbreviations | xix

1   1 Thessalonians 1:1–10: Prescript and Proem | 1
2   1 Thessalonians 2:1–16: Paul and the Thessalonians' Experiences | 10
3   1 Thessalonians 2:17—3:13: Paul's Longing to See Them and News | 20
4   1 Thessalonians 4:1–12: Exhortation | 30
5   1 Thessalonians 4:13–18: The Fate of Those in Christ Who Died | 38
6   1 Thessalonians 5:1–11: Christ's Return for Those Living | 45
7   1 Thessalonians 5:12–28: General Exhortations and Closing | 52
8   2 Thessalonians 1:1–12: Thanksgiving and the Coming Judgment | 59
9   2 Thessalonians 2:1–17: Stand Firm in View of What Is to Come | 68
10 2 Thessalonians 3:1–18: Faithfulness and Against the Disorderly; Closing | 86

Select Bibliography | 97

Introduction

Thessalonica and Paul's Letters

THESSALONICA WAS FOUNDED IN 316–15 BC by Cassander, Alexander the Great's general and Macedonian successor. Cassander named the city after his wife Thessalonice (meaning "the victory of Thessaly"), Alexander's half-sister and the daughter of Philip II.[1] Philip II's capital had been at Pella nearby, but by the time of Cassander's rule Pella no longer enjoyed the same access to the Loudias River and the Aegean Sea. Thessalonica, on the other hand, enjoyed an outstanding natural harbor at the head of the Thermaic Gulf (Gulf of Salonica).[2] In Roman times, the city straddled the second-century BC Via Egnatia (the Egnatian Way), running east to the Hellespont, then Byzantium (Constantinople/Istanbul), and on to Asia Minor, and west to Dyrrachium on the Adriatic Sea, just across from Brundisium in Italy, with the Via Appia to Rome. The road north along the Axius River passed through the Balkans into the Danube region. The climate was good, and the region rich with mineral deposits. The ancients praised Thessalonica as the "metropolis" or "mother of all Macedonia."[3]

Rome annexed Macedonia in 167 BC after the battle of Pydna the year before and divided it into four parts, with Thessalonica the capital of the second district. A citizen assembly (*demos*), a council (*boule*), and politarchs (officials) governed the city. Thessalonica became Macedonia's capital with the reorganization of the province in 148 BC. Inscriptions praise the Roman praetor Metellus as "savior and benefactor" for quelling

---

1. Strabo, *Geogr.* 7, frag. 21, 24; Dionysius of Halicarnassus, *Ant. or.* 1.49.4.
2. Riesner, *Paul's Early Period*, 338.
3. Strabo, *Geogr.* 7, frag. 21; Antipater, *Anth. Pal.* 9.428.

INTRODUCTION

the 146 BC rebellion against Rome.[4] Thessalonica and Rome would subsequently enjoy close relations. Both Caesar and Octavian received divine honors in the city's coinage. Except under Tiberius, Macedonia enjoyed status as a senatorial province not under direct Roman rule (Dio Cassius 60.24.1). Only 2 percent of extant inscriptions from that period are in Latin.[5] The city would have been especially sensitive to its relations with Rome in the aftermath of Tiberius's demotion of the city to an imperial province. The city had been renewed to senatorial provincial status by Claudius only six years before Paul's arrival.[6]

When Paul arrived, he would have witnessed a bustling population, the most populous in Macedonia (Strabo, *Geogr.* 7.7.4).[7] Trade guilds and pagan cults and temples flourished in this transit hub with its heavy immigrant population. Dionysus, one of the oldest deities worshiped there, was popular, judging by coinage and the Golden (or Vardar) Gate with its dedication by "the tribe of Dionysus," one the three tribes that Cassander united to form the city.[8] Paul would counsel the Thessalonians not to get drunk at night, a common occurrence especially in one of the districts of the city named after the god ("Phallus"—a model of which was carried in religious ceremonies to represent the god Dionysus [1 Thess 5:5–8]).[9] Even more popular at Thessalonica than the Dionysus cult was the worship of Cabirus (Kabiros), with a ubiquitous presence in the city in view of the abundance of coins with his image.[10] The Cabirus temple at Thessalonica unfortunately has not yet been found.[11] Cabirus's cult dates at least to the reign of Augustus.[12] Cabirus was a "savior" god who had come back from the dead after his human brothers had slain him—obvious competition for another man-God risen from the dead. (The brothers made the mistake of burying his head at Mount Olympus.) Egyptian

---

4. Edson, "Macedonia," 134.
5. Witherington, *Thessalonians*, 2.
6. Weima, *Thessalonians*, 7.
7. Population estimates range widely, from forty thousand to two hundred thousand.
8. Edson, "Cults of Thessalonica," 160; Edson, "Macedonia"; Evans, "Eschatology and Ethics," 71–73; *IG* 10.2.1.28: "To Dionysus."
9. Donfried, "Cults of Thessalonica," 337–38.
10. Edson, "Cults of Thessalonica," 188–204; Jewett, *Thessalonian Correspondence*, 127–32; note Koester's caution (*Paul and His World*, 40–41); Hendrix, "Thessalonike," 1:25–26.
11. Hendrix, "Thessalonike," 1:27.
12. Edson, "Cults of Thessalonica," 190.

INTRODUCTION

deities were also especially popular (Sarapis, Osiris, Isis, Anubis).[13] The imperial cult and worship of Roma were central to city life as well. By the end of the first century BC under Augustus, a temple was already erected in honor of Julius Caesar.[14] Paul would also have seen a temple to Augustus (*IG* 10.2.31–10.2.32) and a statue of Augustus with his right hand raised like a hero, likely inspiration for his critique of the claim of "peace and security" in 1 Thess 5:3. Bronze coins had the divinized Julius Caesar with "ΘΕΟΣ" (*theos* [god]) on one side and "Augustus, *divi filius*" (son of god), on the other (*IG* 10.2.1.31).[15] The emperor was even deified as the manifestation of Cabirus, many Thessalonians' personal god.[16] As for a Jewish presence in Thessalonica, archaeological evidence is sparse.[17] Philo mentions Jews in the province (*Legat.* 281). They were populous throughout the eastern half of the empire, and a Samaritan synagogue at Thessalonica dates to the third century BC.[18] A late second- or early third-century AD sarcophagus mentions synagogues (plural) and Jewish names associated with each.[19] Paul could well have begun his public evangelization in synagogues (Acts 17:1–9) and with people in the context of his extensive work hours (1 Thess 2:9).[20] In this religiously diverse context dedicated to the emperor and his realm, with Mount Olympus visible fifty miles away, the Christ believers could be bringing down the gods' wrath when they turned from their former patterns of worship and abandoned the imperial cult (1 Thess 1:9). Paul's ministry understandably aroused great opposition (1 Thess 1:6; 2:2, 14–16).

Paul went to Thessalonica after his poor treatment at Philippi (Acts 16:16–40; 1 Thess 2:2). The usual route from Philippi to Thessalonica (ninety-two miles) followed the Via Egnatia, passing through Amphipolis and Appollonia. Paul stayed at Thessalonica long enough to bring gentiles to faith (1 Thess 1:9), receive financial aid from Philippi on more than one occasion (Phil 4:15–16), establish self-sufficiency in his trade labors (1 Thess 2:9; 2 Thess 3:7–9), preach on multiple occasions (imperfect tense; 1 Thess 3:4; 2 Thess 2:5; 3:10), and train church leaders (1 Thess

13. Koester, *Paul and His World*, 46–54.
14. Harrison, *Paul and Imperial Authorities*, 55; Green, *Thessalonians*, 39.
15. Koester, *Paul and His World*, 43–44.
16. Lightfoot, *Biblical Essays*, 257–58.
17. Koester, *Paul and His World*, 56.
18. Jewett, *Thessalonian Correspondence*, 119–20; Koester, *Paul and His World*, 39.
19. Levinskaya, *Diaspora Setting*, 155–56.
20. Hock, *Social Context*, 41–42; Hock, "Workshop," 444–48.

5:12–13).²¹ He had not wanted to leave but was forced out of the city (1 Thess 2:15, 17–20).

In reconstructing the sequence of events leading to 1 and 2 Thessalonians, one should not discount Acts as a historical source.²² Malherbe observes of Acts 17:4: "'Some' of the Jews were persuaded by Paul, the indefinite pronoun in the series indicating that they constituted the least significant" of those impacted by Paul's message.²³ "Nothing in this account of Paul's founding of the church represents the concerns his gospel frequently raised for Jews."²⁴ Luke documents the conflict that Paul experienced with the Jews at Thessalonica, which apparently led to gentile Christ believers forming their own assemblies. Since the church consisted mostly of former idolaters (1 Thess 1:9), Paul does not quote the Jewish Scriptures and alludes to them in only a few places (e.g., 2:4, 16; 4:5, 6, 8; 5:8, 22). He does not address the Jewish law. Proper conduct understandably occupies a more central place in these letters to former pagans than particular doctrinal concerns. They are to avoid sexual immorality (4:3–8), lead quiet lives, and behave properly in the presence of outsiders (4:11–12).

Some have supposed that 2 Thessalonians was the earlier of the two letters. After leaving Thessalonica, news came of doctrinal error (2 Thess 2:2), people not working (3:11), the Christ believers' persecution (1:4), and a letter written in Paul's name (2:2), all of which necessitated a response, 2 Thessalonians.²⁵ This hypothesis, which may be traced to Hugo Grotius in the nineteenth century, was fleshed out by Thomas W. Manson.²⁶ Most recently, Wanamaker took this approach in his commentary.²⁷ In favor of the hypothesis:

(1) Persecution is in the past in 1 Thess 2:14 but in the present in 2 Thess 1:4–7, suggesting that 2 Thessalonians is the earlier letter.

---

21. Weima, *Thessalonians*, 26.

22. Twenty-five elements in Luke's account are confirmed by 1 Thessalonians (Riesner, *Paul's Early Period*, 366–67).

23. Malherbe, *Letters to the Thessalonians*, 58.

24. Malherbe, *Letters to the Thessalonians*, 56.

25. Malherbe, *Letters to the Thessalonians*, 363.

26. Manson, "Thessalonians."

27. Wanamaker, *Thessalonians*, 37–45.

INTRODUCTION

On the other hand, persecutions could have been intermittent and taking place even when 1 Thessalonians was written (2:15; 3:3).[28]

(2) Disorder appears to be a new problem in 2 Thess 3:11–15 but already known in 1 Thess 4:10–12. Nevertheless, the situation might have gotten significantly worse between 1 and 2 Thessalonians, which would explain the difference in description.[29]

(3) A Pauline signature makes sense if 2 Thessalonians is the earlier letter (3:17). On the other hand, that the Thessalonians had received a spurious letter from him *before* his first to them (2 Thess 2:2) is unlikely.[30]

(4) Not needing to be told about the timing of the end in 1 Thess 5:1 makes sense in view of the teaching in 2 Thess 2:1–12, but this too is inconclusive if 1 Thess 5:1 refers to oral teaching rather than a letter. Concerns might have grown by the time of 2 Thessalonians, requiring additional teaching.[31]

(5) "Now about/concerning" in 1 Thess 4:9, 13; 5:1 introduces answers to questions raised earlier by the recipients on the basis of 2 Thess 3:6–15. On the other hand, the situation might well have worsened after 1 Thessalonians.[32] Paul could simply be responding to the issues that arose with these new converts, irrespective of 2 Thessalonians.[33]

Paul relays in 2 Thessalonians that he had *already* taught his new converts about the end (2:5, 14) and the need to work (3:10), and had given them an example (3:7–9). That 2 Thessalonians is the earlier letter is unlikely.

To reconstruct the events after Paul's departure from the city: Paul traveled to Athens, where he was left alone (1 Thess 3:1). Timothy had gone back to the Thessalonians to strengthen their faith (3:1–5). Timothy and Silas had recently returned from Macedonia with good news (Acts 18:5; 1 Thess 3:6). The Thessalonian church's own mission had become known throughout Greece (1 Thess 1:2–10). Lingering issues moved Paul to want to complete what was lacking in their faith, especially

---

28. Best, *Thessalonians*, 42–43; Jewett, *Thessalonian Correspondence*, 24.
29. Jewett, *Thessalonian Correspondence*, 24–25.
30. Malherbe, *Letters to the Thessalonians*, 362.
31. Jewett, *Thessalonian Correspondence*, 25.
32. Witherington, *Thessalonians*, 14–16.
33. Malherbe, *Letters to the Thessalonians*, 362.

regarding proper sexual conduct, love in their community, and the fate of those who had died (3:10; 4:1–8, 9–12, 13–18). The Thessalonian Christ believers' neighbors were apparently slandering Paul's integrity as a preacher (2:1–16). He was writing not long after arriving at Corinth for his eighteen-month stay after Timothy and Silas had rejoined him—thus late AD 50 or early 51 (Acts 17:1—18:17). Silas and Timothy, back from Thessalonica, co-send the letters (1 Thess 1:1; 2 Thess 1:1), with Paul as the primary author. Apparently not long after the first letter, Paul received an alarming report that the Thessalonian church had been shaken by the claim that the day of the Lord had come, and so some were refusing to work (2 Thess 2:2; 3:6–15). The second letter would address these matters in a context of continued suffering and persecution (1:3–12).[34]

Authorship of I and II Thessalonians

Several late first- and early second-century authors allude to 1 Thessalonians.[35] Marcion (ca. 140) included 1 Thessalonians in his canon,[36] as did the Muratorian Canon at the end of the second century. Irenaeus quotes 1 Thess 5:23 (ca. 180; *Haer.* 5.6.1). The Pauline authorship of 1 Thessalonians is undisputed (1:1; 2:18) with the exception, for some, of 1 Thess 2:13–16.[37] The arguments for these verses' inauthenticity have been decisively answered, and the verses are universally attested in the ancient manuscripts.[38]

Early to mid-second-century authors likewise allude to 2 Thessalonians.[39] In the latter half of that century, Irenaeus quotes 2:9 (*Haer.* 3.7.2); Clement of Alexandria, 3:1–2 (*Strom.* 5.3); and Tertullian, 2:4 (*An.* 57) and 1:6–9; 2:3–4, 9–12; 3:10 (*Marc.* 5.16). The Muratorian Canon and Marcion's included it. No one questioned its authorship until J. E. C. Schmidt in 1801, who took the eschatology of 2 Thess 2:1–12 as contradicting 1 Thess

---

34. On persecution at the hands of the unbelieving gentile populace (2:14), see esp. Still, *Conflict*.

35. Did. 16:6 to 1 Thess 4:16 (the sign of the sound of the trumpet); Ignatius, *Rom.* 2.1; *Eph.* 10.1 to 1 Thess 2:4 and 5:17; Shepherd of Hermas, Vis. 3.9.10 to 1 Thess 5:13; and Barn. 21.6 to 1 Thess 4:9.

36. Tertullian, *Marc.* 5.15.

37. Pearson, "1 Thessalonians 2:13–16"; Schmidt, "1 Thess 2:13–16."

38. E.g., Das, *Paul and the Jews*, 128–39.

39. Ignatius, *Rom.* 10.3 to 2 Thess 3:5; Polycarp, *Phil.* 11.3–11.4 to 2 Thess 1:4 and 3:15; Justin Martyr, *Dial.* 110.6 to 2 Thess 2:3–4.

INTRODUCTION

4:13—5:11. In 1903 William Wrede contended that 2 Thessalonians is literally dependent on and mimicking 1 Thessalonians. The most compelling case against Pauline authorship was Trilling's 1972 monograph.[40] Even so, Trilling's case has been heavily criticized.[41] Malherbe in 2000 concluded that the majority accept 2 Thessalonians' authenticity.[42]

Second Thessalonians appears to have a colder, more authoritarian tone, unlike the warmer, personal tone of 1 Thessalonians: (1) Paul is *obliged* to give thanks in 2 Thess 1:3; 2:13 but simply giving thanks in 1 Thess 1:2; 2:13; (2) the strong "we command" in 2 Thess 3:6-15 vs. the softer "we exhort" in 1 Thess 4:1; 5:14; (3) the appeal to tradition in 2 Thess 2:15; 3:6 vs. the family metaphors of infants, a nursing mother, and a father in 1 Thess 2:7, 11. How could Paul write letters so different in tone within such a short time of each other? Second Thessalonians, however, bears affectionate tonal qualities as well. The Thessalonians' faith is not only increasing but abundantly so amid persecution (2 Thess 1:3). Paul feels obligated *out of joy* to give thanks for them (2 Thess 1:3) and boast of them (1:4). He repeatedly calls them his "brothers (and sisters)" at roughly the same rate as 1 Thessalonians, with both letters much higher than the rest of the Pauline corpus.[43] The unique "brothers and sisters loved by God" in 1 Thess 1:4 is matched by the unique "brothers and sisters loved by the Lord" in 2 Thess 2:13 (which also draws on Benjamin's blessing in Deut 33:12 and not just 1 Thessalonians—an unlikely addition for a forger).[44] The Thessalonians had read 1 Thessalonians not long before, and so Paul could assume a cordial relationship that need not be stressed again in his second letter.[45] Even had the second letter borne a colder, more authoritarian tone, one need not conclude that it is pseudonymous. Some at Thessalonica had been duped by a false prophecy that the day of the Lord had come (2 Thess 2:1-12), while others were refusing to work (3:6-15)—which would naturally account for the more serious tone.

40. Trilling, *Untersuchungen*.
41. Marshall, *Thessalonians*, 28-45; Wanamaker, *Thessalonians*, 17-29; Still, *Conflict*, 46-55; Malherbe, *Letters to the Thessalonians*, 364-74; Foster, "Who Wrote 2 Thessalonians"; Weima, *Thessalonians*, 46-54.
42. Malherbe, *Letters to the Thessalonians*, 364.
43. Fee, *Thessalonians*, 239.
44. Fee, *Thessalonians*, 239.
45. Malherbe notes the warmth of 1:3, 4; 2:13; 3:13, 15 (*Letters to the Thessalonians*, 351).

INTRODUCTION

The author of 2 Thessalonians draws attention to the greeting in his own hand, as Paul, and as a customary authenticating sign in *all* his letters (3:17; 1 Cor 16:21; Gal 6:11; Col 4:18; Phlm 19; a secretary in Rom 16:22). He also warns of a false letter as though from us in 2 Thess 2:2. Although some believe that these claims reek of inauthenticity, Paul is emphatic in Gal 6:11 about the large letters with which he wrote, and one would *expect* an authenticating note when faced with the prospect of a fake letter. First Thessalonians does not bear a closing autograph statement (no imitation of the first letter in *that* regard). One may read 2 Thess 3:17 not primarily as authenticating but as emphasizing Paul's own authority against those refusing to work (3:14).

The eschatology of the letters appears contradictory, arguably belying the same author behind both, since 1 Thessalonians posits a sudden, unexpected coming like a thief in the night and 2 Thessalonians anticipates a series of events presaging its coming.[46] A closer reading, however, dispels the supposed contradiction. Paul is clear in 1 Thess 5:2–3 that the Lord's return will be sudden and unexpected for *unbelievers*, whereas believers "know well" what will take place. Believers are not in the dark for that day to surprise them (1 Thess 5:5). They are to live in a way that prepares for their coming salvation (1 Thess 5:9). Likewise in 2 Thess 2:15, the hearers know well what Paul had repeatedly instructed them while with them. They are God's elect (2 Thess 2:13; 1 Thess 5:9). The eschatological differences between the letters appear to be a function of the specific situation as someone claimed Paul's own authority in writing to them (2 Thess 2:2). To cast a sideways glance, a sudden second coming is taught *alongside* signs of that coming in other early Christian literature (e.g., Mark 13:14–37).

First Thessalonians appears, for some, to be functioning as a model in structure, vocabulary, and phrasing for 2 Thessalonians (e.g., 1 Thess 1:6–8//2 Thess 1:4; 1 Thess 2:12–13//2 Thess 2:13–14; 1 Thess 3:11//2 Thess 2:16; 1 Thess 4:1//2 Thess 3:1; 1 Thess 4:1–2//2 Thess 3:6–7; 1 Thess 4:10–12//2 Thess 3:10–12; 1 Thess 5:23//2 Thess 3:16). The relationship, however, need not be attributed to literary dependence.[47] Some are convinced that an unimaginative use of the earlier letter indicates a forger, but the similarities could just as easily be attributed to the writing of 2 Thessalonians not long after the first letter. Further, the case for

---

46. E.g., Menken, *2 Thessalonians*, 28–30.
47. Marshall, *Thessalonians*, 28–45; Wanamaker, *Thessalonians*, 17–28.

INTRODUCTION

inauthenticity suffers from claiming that 2 Thessalonians is too much like 1 Thessalonians and yet at the same time too different.[48] For instance, the thanksgiving sections in both letters introduce a major item for the respective letter: Paul's past relationships with the recipients in 1 Thessalonians and the impending divine judgment of the persecutors in 2 Thessalonians. Surely the second letter would mirror more closely the first.[49] The differences may be attributed to the changed situation since the first letter. Finally, 2 Thessalonians parallels only 1 Thessalonians, and yet one would expect parallels to *other* Pauline letters were it a later, post-Pauline production.[50]

A pseudonymous 2 Thessalonians is unlikely for other reasons as well. What historical context would lead someone to take up the same subjects from 1 Thessalonians of persecution, confusion about the timing of the day of the Lord, and idle church members thirty years later to a non-Thessalonian church after Paul's death?[51] Further, the author refers to "*the* temple of *the* God" in 2 Thess 2:4, and yet the Jerusalem temple had been destroyed by the time of a later, pseudonymous letter. Surely a later forger would not want to assume the temple's *continued* existence, especially after its destruction.[52] Pseudonymous authorship, while common in apocalypses, is rare in ancient *letters*.[53] The early Christians were rather critical of pseudonymity.[54] Recipients of a new letter in the name of Paul decades later would have been skeptical upon its sudden appearance, especially when addressed to the same church as an earlier, authentic letter.[55] "[The hypothesis] also assumes that while the pseudonymous author (and the modern scholar) could discern the differences between the two letters, the original readers could not."[56] Polycarp is drawing on 2 Thessalonians as Pauline by the early second century (*Phil.* 11.3-4: 2 Thess 1:4; 3:15; ca. AD 110). Ultimately, as John M. G. Barclay and

48. See Malherbe's helpful chart (*Letters to the Thessalonians*, 356–58).

49. Fee, *Thessalonians*, 239. "There are similarities between the two letters, but they are not as great as is frequently thought, and they differ in importance" (Malherbe, *Letters to the Thessalonians*, 357).

50. Fee, *Thessalonians*, 240.

51. Malherbe, *Letters to the Thessalonians*, 373–74.

52. Witherington, *Thessalonians*, 12–13; also Rigaux, *Thessaloniciens*, 144–45.

53. Carson and Moo, *Introduction*, 541; Witherington, *Thessalonians*, 11, 23. Epistle of Barnabas is a likely candidate.

54. Wilder, *Pseudonymity*, 35–73, esp. 62.

55. Malherbe, *Letters to the Thessalonians*, 373–74.

56. Malherbe, *Letters to the Thessalonians*, 374.

others have contended, the second letter evinces a situation that makes good sense not long after the first letter.[57]

The Letters' Contents

Paul appeared before the Roman proconsul Gallio's tribunal in the summer of AD 51, at the end of an eighteen-month stay in the city of Corinth.[58] That places Paul's arrival at Corinth in late 49 or very early 50 after leaving Thessalonica a few months earlier, with stops at Berea and Athens along the way (Acts 17–18). He penned the first letter just after arriving in Corinth when Silas and Timothy rejoined him, bringing news from the congregation (Acts 18:1, 5; 1 Thess 3:1–2, 6). Paul's labors in Thessalonica were therefore in the fall of 49 and 1 Thessalonians in late spring 50. Second Thessalonians would have been only a few weeks or months after the first letter.

Paul's frequent references to his original preaching at Thessalonica permit reconstruction of his missionary proclamation, especially since it had not been long since his visit. He had proclaimed the death and resurrection of Jesus, God's Son "for us" (1 Thess 4:14; 5:10), but within an apocalyptic context awaiting Jesus's imminent return (1:10) with the saints (3:13).[59] The sudden events would take the children of darkness by surprise (5:1–11), inflicting wrath on those "others" proclaiming their false "peace and security" (5:2–3), but sparing Christ's own (1:10; 5:9) who had left their idols behind (1:9). His message was replete with the typical dualisms of Jewish apocalyptic thought: heaven vs. earth, present vs. future, and the elect (1:4) vs. the lost. Thanks to Jesus's death and resurrection, the Thessalonians were situated right at the turning point of the ages, and Paul writes to encourage blameless and holy behavior (e.g., 3:13; 4:1–3) fitting for their newfound identity.

With such expectations, the congregation was likely surprised when some of their own began to die (1 Thess 4:13–18). The warm tone of the letter suggests that the Thessalonians had never wavered in their anticipation

---

57. Barclay, "Conflict," 525–29.
58. For the timing, see Das, *Galatians*, 43–45.
59. This brief sketch is indebted to Barclay, "Conflict"; Barclay, "Thessalonica and Corinth," esp. 49–56. Apocalypses and their worldview became popular after the persecution of the Jewish people under Antiochus IV Epiphanes in 167 BC until Hadrian's destruction of the Jewish nation in AD 135, a roughly three-hundred-year period. Paul shares this worldview.

of Christ's return (4:15, 17) but were grieving that their loved ones had missed the wonderful events soon to come. They were restlessly impatient for that return to take place (5:1–11). Although the letter is full of reminders of what the Thessalonians already know, even to the point of saying that a letter is not necessary (1:4; 2:1, 2, 5, 9, 10, 11; 3:3b–4; 4:1, 2, 6, 10, 11; 5:1), 4:13 uniquely turns to something the Thessalonians do *not* already know. Paul shares a message of comfort that those who have died will not miss the events to come at Christ's return but rather will be enjoying those events firsthand and even *before* those who are alive who are left (4:15–17).

The Thessalonian social context was one of conflict and persecution, which had begun already when Paul was present (Acts 17; 1 Thess 2:2). Some had apparently slandered Paul's preaching as springing from impure motives (1 Thess 2:3–12). After his departure, the Thessalonians likewise experienced afflictions and persecution (1:6; 2:14). Paul had been so concerned by this that he had sent Timothy back to check on them (3:3), even though he had already forewarned them that this would happen (3:4). He does not point to anyone having died as a result of this persecution (potentially the ultimate example of Christ-likeness). The parallels with Paul's own persecution and with Jesus's crucifixion (1:6; 2:15–16) indicate that the persecution had nevertheless been vigorous and not merely mental distress (*thlipsis* [3:7]). The Thessalonians had abandoned their worship of the gods in a city that enjoyed close relations with Rome and its cult (1:9). They were likely drawing their neighbors' attention as they advocated a "Savior" God who seemed less of a Savior, having died on a cross a few decades earlier, than the time-tested local favorite, Cabirus. The deaths in their congregation took place only a few weeks or months since Paul's visit. The gods would not have been pleased by the Christ believers. One can imagine the resentment, mockery, slander, and ostracism.

Perhaps an aggressive approach to sharing the message of their newfound faith had drawn negative attention. The Thessalonians would have had models in the aggressive, fraudulent Cynic street preachers (runaway slaves?), which may explain Paul's elaboration on his own approach to evangelizing (1 Thess 2:1–12). They are not to return evil for evil (5:15) and are to live quietly, minding their own affairs (4:11–12). Were some choosing to stop working in order to take their message to the people of their city (1:8)? Paul himself would occasionally sound like a street preacher with his litany of this world's immorality (Rom 1:18–32; 1 Cor 6:9–11; 1 Thess 4:5; 5:7).

INTRODUCTION

The more the Thessalonians suffered for their faith, the more that would have reinforced a sense of social alienation, as they divided the world into "us" and "them." Those not confessing the same Christ-centered beliefs were "outsiders" (1 Thess 4:12), the "rest" of humanity (4:13; 5:6). Such people do not know God (4:5) and are children of darkness, who merely sleep and get drunk (5:7) with no hope (4:13). With the whole world caught up in this cosmic conflict, even Satan stands opposed to the early Christ believers (2:18). Ironically, Paul makes these claims as one recently arrived in Macedonia from foreign shores; he is redrawing their social map to bind them closer to other Christ believers, even as far away as Judea (2:14–15), let alone the distant reaches of Greece and Macedonia (1:7; 4:10). In a world where the majority never travel that far from where they were born and raised, such distant Christ believers are their true brothers, sisters, and family, and not those closest to them outside the fledgling faith. Social alienation would reinforce a sense that they are the ones destined for salvation and vindication. As for those who died, Paul writes a letter of hope that they have not missed out (4:13–18). Perhaps not too much should be read into Timothy's report of their faith and love in 3:6 and not the full triad of faith, love, *and hope* (1:3; 5:8), but Paul's letter would have encouraged hope for what is to come.

Turning to 2 Thessalonians, the church of God's chosen (2 Thess 2:14–16) was still undergoing intense persecution (1:4–9). Their apocalyptic expectations had reached a feverish pitch with some proclaiming "the day of the Lord" as already arrived (a day of wrath according to 1 Thess 5:2–3). Were some pointing to recent events as proof that that day had come? Tacitus relays that a series of earthquakes had rocked Macedonia in AD 51–52, potentially devastating in a world where buildings were not often built that could withstand the sudden shaking. *Any* devastating event, however, could have been interpreted this way (famine, plague). What better situation for Paul's Second Letter to the Thessalonians than not long after the first letter when, within a few weeks or months, Paul's apocalyptic chickens had come home to roost. Now Paul must admonish those who have abandoned jobs in the face of the imminent coming of the end to go back to work (3:6–13). More is yet to come, especially the man of lawlessness (2:1–12). God's wrath will *eventually* express itself against those persecuting them (1:6, 8, 9; 2:10–12). In the meanwhile, they should adopt a more balanced perspective, return to work, and not interfere in the business of others (3:6–15).

Abbreviations

Scripture Abbreviations

Hebrew Bible/Old Testament

Gen	Genesis
Exod	Exodus
Lev	Leviticus
Num	Numbers
Deut	Deuteronomy
Josh	Joshua
Judg	Judges
1 Sam	1 Samuel
2 Sam	2 Samuel
1 Kgs	1 Kings
1 Chr	1 Chronicles
2 Chr	2 Chronicles
Neh	Nehemiah
Ps (pl. Pss)	Psalm (pl. Psalms)
Prov	Proverbs
Isa	Isaiah
Jer	Jeremiah

ABBREVIATIONS

Ezek	Ezekiel
Dan	Daniel
Hos	Hosea
Obad	Obadiah
Mic	Micah
Hab	Habakkuk
Zeph	Zephaniah
Zech	Zechariah
Mal	Malachi

New Testament

Matt	Matthew
Rom	Romans
1 Cor	1 Corinthians
2 Cor	2 Corinthians
Gal	Galatians
Eph	Ephesians
Phil	Philippians
Col	Colossians
1 Thess	1 Thessalonians
2 Thess	2 Thessalonians
1 Tim	1 Timothy
2 Tim	2 Timothy
Phlm	Philemon
Heb	Hebrews
Jas	James
1 Pet	1 Peter
2 Pet	2 Peter
Rev	Revelation

Abbreviations

Apocryphal/Deuterocanonical Books

Add Esth	Additions to Esther
Wis	Wisdom of Solomon
Sir	Sirach
1 Macc	1 Maccabees
2 Macc	2 Maccabees
4 Macc	4 Maccabees

Other Ancient Sources

2 Bar.	2 Baruch
1 En.	1 Enoch
2 En.	2 Enoch
3 En.	3 Enoch
Jos. Asen.	Joseph and Aseneth
Jub.	Jubilees
T. Ash.	Testament of Asher
T. Benj.	Testament of Benjamin
T. Isaac	Testament of Isaac
T. Iss.	Testament of Issachar
T. Jos.	Testament of Joseph
T. Jud.	Testament of Judah
T. Naph	Testament of Naphtali
T. Reu.	Testament of Reuben

Ambrose

Exc.	*De excessu fratris sui Satyri*

Antipater

Anth. Pal.	*Anthologia Palatina*

ABBREVIATIONS

Apoc. Mos. Apocalypse of Moses

Aristotle
Eth. nic.   *Ethica nicomachea*
Rhet.   *Rhetorica*

Athanasius
C. Ar.   *Orationes contra Arianos*
H. Ar.   *Historia Arianorum*

Augustine
Catech.   *De catechizandis rudibus*
Civ.   *De civitate Dei*
Corrept.   *De correptione et gratia*
Enarrat. Ps. *Enarrationes in Psalmos*
Enchir.   *Enchiridion de fide, spe, et caritate*
Fid. op.   *De fide et operibus*
Grat.   *De gratia et libero arbitrio*
Op. mon.   *De opere monachorum*
Nupt.   *De nuptiis et concupiscentia ad Valerium comitem*
Praed.   *De praedestinatione sanctorum*
Serm.   *Sermones*
Tract. Ev. Jo. *In Evangelium Johannis tractatus*

Barn.   Barnabas

Cicero
Att.   *Epistulae ad Atticum*
Cael.   *Pro Caelio*
De or. *De oratore*

| *Tusc.* | *Tusculanae disputationes* |

Clement of Alexandria

Paed.	*Paedagogus*
Strom.	*Stromateis*
Const. ap.	Apostolic Constitutions

Dead Sea Scrolls

1QH	Thanksgiving Hymns
1QM	War Scroll
1QpHab	Pesher Habakkuk
1QS	Rule of the Community
CD	Cairo Genizah copy of the Damascus Document

Demosthenes

| *3 Olynth.* | *Olynthiaca iii* |
| [*Neaer.*] | *In Neaeram* |

Did.   Didache

Dio Chrysostom

Alex.	*Ad Alexandrinos (Or. 32)*
Avar.	*De avaritia (Or. 17)*
Lib.	*De libertate (Or. 80)*
Ven.	*Venator (Or. 7)*

Diodorus Siculus

| *Bib. hist.* | *Bibliotheca historica* |

Diogenes Laertius

| *Vit.* | *Vita* |

ABBREVIATIONS

Dionysius of Halicarnassus
Ant. or.   *De antiquis oratoribus*
Ant. rom.   *Antiquitates romanae*

Epictetus
Diatr.   *Diatribai (Dissertationes)*

Eusebius
Hist. eccl.   *Historia ecclesiastica*

Euripides
Iph. taur.   *Iphigenia taurica*

Hippolytus
Comm. Dan. *Commentarium in Danielem*
Trad. ap.   *Traditio apostolica*

Homer
Il.   *Ilias*

Horace
Sat.   *Satirae*

Ignatius
Eph.   *To the Ephesians*
Pol.   *To Polycarp*
Rom.   *To the Romans*

Irenaeus
Haer.   *Adversus haereses (Elenchos)*

Isocrates
Demon.   *Ad Demonicum (Or. 1)*

ABBREVIATIONS

Jerome
Vigil.	*Adversus Vigilantium*

Josephus
A.J.	*Antiquitates judaicae*
B.J.	*Bellum judaicum*

Julian
Ep.	*Epistulae*

Justin Martyr
1 Apol.	*Apologia i*
Dial.	*Dialogus cum Tryphone*

Lucian
Icar.	*Icaromenippus*
Mart. Isa.	Martyrdom and Ascension of Isaiah 1–5
MT	Masoretic Text

Origen
Cels.	*Contra Celsum*
Comm. Matt.	*Commentarium in evangelium Matthaei*
Or.	*De oratione (Peri proseuchēs)*
Princ.	*De principiis (Peri archōn)*
P.Oxy.	Oxyrhynchus papyri

Philo
Flacc.	*In Flaccum*
Legat.	*Legatio ad Gaium*

Plutarch
Ant.	*Antonius*

ABBREVIATIONS

Conj. praec.   *Conjugalia Praecepta*
Mor.   *Moralia*

Polybius
Hist.   *Histories*

Polycarp
Phil.   *To the Philippians*
Ps.-Phoc.   Pseudo-Phocylides
Pss. Sol.   Psalms of Solomon

Quintilian
Inst.   *Institutio oratoria*

Seneca
Ep.   *Epistulae morales*

Shepherd of Hermas
Mand.   Mandate(s)
Vis.   Vision(s)
Sib. Or.   Sibylline Oracle(s)

Sophocles
El.   *Elektra*

Strabo
Geogr.   *Geographica*

Tacitus
Hist.   *Historiae*

Tatian
Or. Graec.   *Oratio ad Graecos* (*Pros Hellēnas*)

Tertullian

An.	*De anima*
Apol.	*Apologeticus*
Idol.	*De idololatria*
Marc.	*Adversus Marcionem*
Pat.	*De patientia*
Pud.	*De pudicitia*
Res.	*De resurrectione carnis*

Theocritus

Id.	*Idylls*

Xenophon

Cyr.	*Cyropaedia*
Hier.	*Hiero*

Abbreviations of Reference Works

AB	Anchor Bible
ANF	The Ante-Nicene Fathers. Edited by Alexander Roberts and James Donaldson. 1885–87. 10 vols. Repr., Peabody, MA: Hendrickson, 1994
ANTC	Abingdon New Testament Commentaries
BECNT	Baker Exegetical Commentary on the New Testament
BETL	Bibliotheca Ephemeridum Theologicarum Lovaniensium
BBR	*Bulletin for Biblical Research*
BZNW	Beihefte zur Zeitschrift für die neutestamentliche Wissenschaft
CBQ	*Catholic Biblical Quarterly*
ConBNT	Coniectanea Neotestamentica or Coniectanea Biblica: New Testament Series

ABBREVIATIONS

ConC	Concordia Commentary
FC	Fathers of the Church
HNTC	Harper's New Testament Commentaries
HTR	*Harvard Theological Review*
IG	*Inscriptiones Graecae. Editio Minor.* Berlin: de Gruyter, 1924–
JBL	*Journal of Biblical Literature*
JETS	*Journal of the Evangelical Theological Society*
JSNT	*Journal for the Study of the New Testament*
JSNTSup	Journal for the Study of the New Testament Supplement Series
JTS	*Journal of Theological Studies*
LCC	Library of Christian Classics
LCL	Loeb Classical Library
LEC	Library of Early Christianity
NAC	New American Commentary
NCB	New Century Bible
NICNT	New International Commentary on the New Testament
NIGTC	New International Greek Testament Commentary
NovT	*Novum Testamentum*
NPNF[1]	*A Select Library of Nicene and Post-Nicene Fathers of the Christian Church.* Edited by Philip Schaff. 1st ser. 14 vols. 1886–89. Repr., Peabody, MA: Hendrickson, 1994
NPNF[2]	*A Select Library of Nicene and Post-Nicene Fathers of the Christian Church.* Edited by Philip Schaff and Henry Wace. 2nd ser. 14 vols. 1890–1900. Repr., Peabody, MA: Hendrickson, 1994
NTL	New Testament Library
NTS	*New Testament Studies*

ABBREVIATIONS

OGIS	*Orientis Graeci Inscriptiones Selectae*. Edited by Wilhelm Dittenberger. 2 vols. Leipzig: Hirzel, 1903–5
PGM	*Papyri Graecae Magicae: Die griechischen Zauberpapyri*. Edited by Karl Preisendanz. 2nd ed. Stuttgart: Teubner, 1973–74
SBLSBS	Society of Biblical Literature Sources for Biblical Study
SEG	Supplementum epigraphicum graecum
SNTSMS	Society for New Testament Studies Monograph Series
SP	Sacra Pagina
ST	*The Summa Theologica*. By Thomas Aquinas. 2 vols. 2nd ed. Great Books of the Western World 17–18. Translated by Laurence Shapcote. Chicago: Encyclopedia Britannica, 1990
TS	Texts and Studies
WBC	Word Biblical Commentary
WGRW	Writings from the Greco-Roman World
WTJ	*Westminster Theological Journal*
WUNT	Wissenschaftliche Untersuchungen zum Neuen Testament

I

1 Thessalonians 1:1–10
Prescript and Proem

Translation

[1] PAUL AND SILVANUS and Timothy to the assembly of the Thessalonians in God the Father and the Lord Jesus Christ, grace to you and peace.

[2] We are always giving thanks to God for all of you, constantly making mention of you in our prayers, [3] because we remember your work of faith and labor of love and endurance of hope in the Lord Jesus Christ before our God and Father, [4] since we know, brothers and sisters loved by God, your election. [5] For our gospel has not only come to you in word but also in power and in the Holy Spirit and with much conviction, just as you know what sort of persons we became among you for your sake. [6] And so you yourselves became imitators of us and of the Lord, when you received the word amid much affliction with the joy of the Holy Spirit, [7] so that you became an example for all the believers in Macedonia and in Achaia. [8] For the word of the Lord has sounded forth from you not only in Macedonia and in Achaia, but your faith before God has spread to every place, so that we have no need to say anything. [9] For they themselves are reporting about us what kind of visit we had among you, and how you turned to God from idols, in order to serve a living and true God [10] and to wait for his Son from the heavens, whom he raised from the dead, Jesus, who rescues us from the coming wrath.

Commentary

The standard Greco-Roman epistolary prescript in antiquity consisted of sender(s), addressee, and greetings. Paul typically identifies co-sender(s), who might have helped in the composition. The Thessalonian correspondence is unique in v. 1 with *three* co-senders, and Paul's "we" reinforces their joint activity. Multiple co-senders in ancient letters is rare. The "we" often interchanges with "I" (1 Thess 2:18; 3:2, 5), identifying Paul as the main author. He speaks in his own name in 5:27. Thus the three are likely co-senders rather than co-authors, but with a sense of unanimity and authority behind the document (note the need for multiple witnesses in Num 35:30; Deut 19:15). Their collective authority stands behind the letter. Paul may be reinforcing Timothy's authority as a teacher at Thessalonica (3:2–3), if not also Silvanus's (Acts 17:1–9 [Silas]; 2 Cor 1:19).[1]

The seventeenth-century Matthew Poole explained that Paul's not identifying himself as an apostle was because Thessalonica was free of false apostles or of anyone who might question his credentials.[2] The early verses of 1 Thessalonians offer no hint of resistance or tension with Paul, as the unembellished list of co-senders also suggests.

"Paul" means "short" and sounds like the Hebrew "Saul," his Jewish name (e.g., Acts 9:4). The Greek name would be preferable since "Saul" in Greek meant walking like a prostitute. Paul does not mention the latter name. "Silvanus" is the latinized form of "Silus," itself likely the *Aramaic* form of the Hebrew "Saul." If so, the two shared the same Hebrew name. The book of Acts describes Silas's missionary role alongside Paul (Acts 15–18). As for Timothy, Paul had brought him to faith (1 Cor 4:15–17), and Acts narrates his missionary role as well (Acts 16–17; also 1 Thess 3:1–6). As a founding missionary, Paul sent him back to check on the congregation.

Paul addresses "assemblies" in his early letters (Gal 1:2; 1 Cor 1:2; 2 Cor 1:1; 2 Thess 1:1).[3] He does not refer here, as he does elsewhere in his letters, to the Christian gathering in a particular location, but rather to a gathering of *people*. (The translation "church" would be anachronistic.) Paul intended the letter be read aloud in their corporate gathering. Their assembly parallels the gathering of Israel (e.g., Deut 4:10; 1 Kgs 8:14 LXX), as opposed to the larger Thessalonian *public* assembly in

---

1. Kim and Bruce, *Thessalonians*, 124–25.
2. Poole, *Commentary*, 3:731.
3. Kim and Bruce, *Thessalonians*, 126.

the *polis* with a different fate than those under their new "Lord" (Jesus Christ; former pagans [1 Thess 1:9; 4:5]).[4] The venerable Bede (ca. 673–735) followed Augustine in noting how Paul uses a different word for Christian gatherings than the Jews' (*convocatio/ekklēsia* vs. *congregatio/synagogue*).[5]

The Thessalonian Christ-believing assembly was "in God the Father and the Lord Jesus Christ" (also Acts 17:28), whether this is spatial/sphere, in communion with God and Christ—or instrumental, by God's action through Christ (similarly 1 Thess 2:2). The nineteenth-century commentator Hermann Olshausen observed that "in God the Father" is unique to 1 and 2 Thessalonians.[6] The two epistles stress God more than any other Pauline letter except for Romans. Paul often juxtaposes God the Father and the Lord Jesus Christ (note the single preposition here) and ascribes parallel actions to each (e.g., 1 Cor 7:17–24; 8:5–6; 2 Cor 13:13; 2 Thess 2:16). The one God has been reconceptualized to include reference also to the "Lord" Jesus Christ (e.g., 1 Cor 8:6). Mention in the immediately ensuing verses of God the Father, the Lord Jesus Christ, and the Holy Spirit prompted Basil the Great (ca. 330–79) to compare the three coworkers sending this letter to the coequal Trinity with all three working together for one purpose.[7]

The people of this provincial capital would likely notice that the Roman emperor is not here the Father or Lord, and in *this* assembly are matters of *eternal* significance. *This* Father and Lord bring grace and peace (the Greek equivalent of the Hebrew *shalom*) in a modified hellenized Jewish greeting. "Grace" (*charis*) replaces the standard Hellenistic letter greeting, *chairein*, from the same word group. Paul will close the letter with "peace" and "grace" as well (1 Thess 5:23, 28).

The prescript (1 Thess 1:1) is typically followed in Greco-Roman letters by a proem or exordium (1:2–10) expressing thanks for the addressees' well-being (Rom 1:8–15; 1 Cor 1:4–9; Phil 1:3–11; Col 1:3–14; 2 Thess 1:3–12; Phlm 4–7). The prescript and proem signal the key themes of the letter: the Thessalonians' love (1 Thess 1:3; 3:6, 12; 4:9), their hope (1:3; 4:13—5:11), their conversion (1:10—2:12), salvation (1:10; 5:9), election and calling (1:4; 2:12; 4:7; 5:24), their enduring persecution

---

4. Kim and Bruce, *Thessalonians*, 129–31. On public assemblies, see Josephus, *A.J.* 12.4.2 §164.

5. Bede the Venerable, *Excerpts*, 285.

6. Olshausen, *Commentary*, 403.

7. Basil the Great, *On the Spirit* 25.59 (*NPNF*[2] 8:37); *Letter* 210.4 (*NPNF*[2] 8:250).

(1:6; 2:14–16), God's wrath (1:10; 2:16; 4:6; 5:9), and Christ's impending return (1:10; 4:13—5:11). Where the proem ends and the letter's body begins is unclear. Paul gives thanks in 2:13 and 3:9 as well (potentially *three* thanksgiving subsections). A new (second?) section of the letter is more clearly demarcated in 4:1, Paul's exhortation. First Thessalonians 1:2–10 represents a coherent unit of thought, whether construed as a single sentence or more.

Paul opens with a prayer thanking God for the Thessalonians (1 Thess 1:2), consistent with his practice to regularly pray for them. He wants to make an initial, rhetorical impression with the repeated and reverent (even liturgical) *p* sound as the letter is read (alliteration in the Greek).[8] He closes the letter, framing it, by asking them to pray for him as well (5:25). E. M. Bounds in his classic on prayer often commented on how Paul modeled a persistent, devotional life of prayer, given his frequent shifts to praying with his addressees, as in this verse.[9] Paul thanks God for them *all* (elsewhere only in Rom 1:4, 8), signaling his love and concern for *each* of them in the midst of persecution.

Verse 3 continues the sentence. "We remember" is the first in a series throughout the letter as Paul reminds the Thessalonians of what they have already learned, know, and believe, what is undisputed common ground (1:4; 2:1, 8, 9, 10, 11; 3:3–4; 4:1, 2, 6, 10, 11; 5:1). They are to "stand" their ground (3:8). Paul here reverses the order of God our Father and the Lord Jesus Christ from v. 1. The sandwiched "constantly" could go with either "making mention" in prayer (see 5:17) or "we remember your work" and may be sandwiched to make a *two*fold point. Thanks are due God, not the Thessalonians, for what God has done among them ("God": nineteen times by 2:15!).

Faith, love, and hope are a Pauline triad and perhaps even pre-Pauline (Rom 5:1–5; 1 Cor 13:13; Gal 5:5–6; Eph 4:2–5; Col 1:4–5; also Heb 6:10–12; 10:22–24; 1 Pet 1:3–8; 1:21–22). Early Christians noted the faith-hope-love triad early on (e.g., Polycarp, *Phil.* 3.2–3). Faith consists of loyalty and is not simply "belief."[10] "Love" is what God poured out on humanity in Christ (Rom 5:5; 8:39; 2 Cor 13:13; 2 Thess 3:5) and is now expressed by believers toward each other (1 Thess 4:9). Faith, hope, and love have produced their work, labor, and perseverance (also 1 Cor

---

8. *Pantote peri pantōn . . . poioumenoi . . . proseuchōn . . . adialeiptōs* (always for all . . . making . . . prayers . . . constantly) (Malherbe, *Letters to the Thessalonians*, 106–7).

9. Bounds, *Essentials of Prayer*.

10. Morgan, *Roman Faith*.

13:13; Col 1:4–5). This is not a work that is producing faith, but rather the reverse, even as Christlike love likewise expresses itself in hard work or labor for others (note the idleness Paul combats in 1 Thess 5:14). Faith and love are *active*. Although Paul combats the notion that one may be saved by works elsewhere (e.g., Galatians), he nevertheless views works as an important and necessary expression of faith. Climaxing the triadic list is the hope that inspires endurance, grounded specifically in the Lord Jesus and his impending return (4:13–5:11; whereas love is climactic in 1 Cor 13:13). Although Paul will be writing about events to come in chs. 4 and 5, the first three chapters remain focused on such day-to-day matters as work, suffering, consoling, encouraging, and the good news.[11]

"In the Lord Jesus Christ" may modify the entire triad, as perhaps does "before our God and Father"—assuming the latter does not modify the more distant "we remember," thus sandwiching what is between. Paul is further emphasizing hope since what takes place in the Lord Jesus Christ also takes place in the presence of God (also 1 Thess 2:19; 3:13; 2 Cor 5:10). "*Before* God our Father" recognizes God *their* Father as the coming Judge (also 1 Thess 1:9–10; 3:13; 5:9).[12] Christ is already dwelling in glory before the Father, even as the Thessalonians will one day dwell before both Christ and the Father.

Paul's address of them as "brothers and sisters" (v. 4) redraws their social map, bringing them into a relationship with a *new* family, all the children of God the Father (vv. 1, 3), a common Pauline motif, but especially in 1 and 2 Thessalonians with the highest density of instances in the Pauline Letters: twenty-one times. The address of the "brothers and sisters" at this point draws attention to and reinforces their identity as God's elect, a matter about which Paul is confident ("knows").

Shared suffering in the midst of persecution by those outside their assembly (see v. 6) would bond the Thessalonians to each other. This assembly has become their *real* family! They are children to Paul (1 Thess 2:7), even as he has been "orphaned" from them (2:17). More importantly, like Israel, they are "loved" by God (Pss 60:5 [59:7 LXX]; 108:6 [107:7]). God's historic actions on behalf of his people are now on behalf of the Thessalonians! Paul is proclaiming a new *identity* for the Thessalonians and (comfortingly) reminding them of God's continued activity on their behalf—all a function of their belief in Christ.

---

11. Witherington, *Thessalonians*, 63.
12. Kim and Bruce, *Thessalonians*, 147–48.

What the Thessalonians enjoy begins with God's election and love. The Thessalonians may be congratulated for their faith, hope, and love (1:3); their endurance of persecution (1:6–7); and their conversion (1:9–10), all of which stem from God's work in election (1:4), and so God is to be thanked. Election had been the prerogative of Israel in the Scriptures (e.g., Deut 4:37; 7:6; 1 Kgs 3:8; Isa 44:2; Hos 2:23), and yet this prerogative is now claimed for the gentile Thessalonians. This election has brought them to faith, as v. 5 explains, and it came through Paul's preaching to them not only in word but also in power and in the Holy Spirit and much conviction. First and Second Thessalonians are unique in the Pauline corpus in emphasizing election and calling (election [1 Thess 1:4–5; 5:9; 2 Thess 2:13]; calling [1 Thess 2:12; 4:7; 5:23–24; 2 Thess 1:11; 2:14]). In a time of trial, such language is comforting. Nevertheless, Paul still admonishes them against apostasy (1 Thess 3:5), even as God protects the assembly (1 Thess 5:23; 2 Thess 2:3) and is faithful (1 Thess 5:24; 2 Thess 3:3).[13] Thomas Aquinas, long before the Reformation, traced election to God's unmerited grace: "Nobody has been so insane as to say that merit is the cause of divine predestination as regards the act of the predestinator"; God *chose* to save.[14] Early Christian authors traced growth and life in the faith to the power of God, e.g., the fourth-century Chrysostom: "God also is thanked for them, as Himself having done it all."[15]

Paul is likely explaining in v. 5 *how* he "knows" they were chosen: causal rather than an epexegetical "that is" or "namely." The gospel he and his companions preached had worked powerfully among them (it is "of God" in 1 Thess 2:2, 8, 9!). The "gospel" (or "good news") is a Pauline favorite (over sixty times in his letters) and might have originated in the Jerusalem church (or even with Jesus), reflecting Isa 40:9; 52:7; 61:1–2 (also in Luke 4:18). The Thessalonians would have been familiar with Roman imperial propaganda and its "good news" of Caesar's benefactions (e.g., the Priene inscription of 9 BC). The gospel message is so powerful that it has, by the working of the Holy Spirit, created a change in the lives of the Thessalonians. The power of the Spirit worked not only "with much conviction" (note Paul's boldness in 1 Thess 2:2) but also accompanied by signs and wonders (e.g., Rom 15:19, and the *inclusio* with prophetic utterances of the Spirit in 1 Thess 5:19–20). Paul was clearly no charlatan popular philosopher.

13. Witherington, *Thessalonians*, 64.
14. *ST* 1, q. 23, art. 5; also art. 3.
15. John Chrysostom, *Homilies on 1 Thessalonians* 2 (on 1:2) (*NPNF*[1] 13:324).

Paul turns from the gospel message to the gospel's messengers at the end of v. 5. He reminds them of his manner of life in their midst, a matter to which he will return in 1 Thess 2:9-10. The Thessalonians already "know" the sorts of persons Paul and his companions were among them. Paul is already preparing for the defense of his preaching and character in 2:1-16.

This verse offers the first of the many expressions of what the Thessalonians "know" (1 Thess 2:1-2, 5, 11; 3:3, 4; 4:2; 5:2), although see v. 3's reminder. Reminders among teachers of philosophy served to strengthen the students' commitment to what they had been taught (e.g., Seneca, *Ep.* 11.9). This powerful gospel was what they recognized already when Paul was first preaching to them (and not just retrospectively).[16]

Now, with vv. 6-7, Paul turns to how the Thessalonians received the gospel message. The emphatic "you yourselves" was presaged by the doubled "you" in the prior verse (note the "and" connecting these verses to 1 Thess 1:2-5). Paul places himself before the Lord here likely because he is about to launch into a defense of his ministry style in a few verses (ch. 2).

The Thessalonians have become imitators of Paul and of Jesus, another major Pauline motif (1 Cor 2:2; 4:16-17; 7:7-8; 11:1; Gal 4:12-20; Phil 1:30; 2:5-11; 3:17; 4:9; 1 Thess 2:14). The ancients encouraged the imitation of great people and of great teachers (e.g., Isocrates, *Demon.* 4.11; Seneca, *Ep.* 6.5 [people trust their eyes more than their ears]; 7.6-9; 11.8-10; 52.8; 104.20-33; Quintilian, *Inst.* 10.2.1-28). Christ is the perfect example, and Paul is imitating Christ (1 Cor 11:1). The Thessalonians are to imitate both. Actually, this is not an exhortation but rather a reminder of what the Thessalonians have *already* done (an indicative vs. the usual imperatives in Paul to imitate). Even more, the Thessalonians did this in the face of persecution (1 Thess 3:3; 2 Thess 1:4, imitating the persecuted Judeans in 1 Thess 2:13-16).

The persecution here does not refer merely to internal distress, since Jesus, their model, is not identified as suffering in that way. This is genuine persecution—but suffering to be expected given the end of time, and likely entailing also internal anxiety and distress. Paul celebrates joy in the midst of persecution for their newfound convictions (1 Thess 1:6). The Thessalonians are not to be surprised by this suffering (3:2-3). They are to rejoice always (5:16-18). This joy is evidence of the Spirit's invasion of their lives (note the Spirit's "fruit" elsewhere in Gal 5:22). The

---

16. Kim and Bruce, *Thessalonians*, 154-55.

Thessalonians are being watched, in two Roman provinces at that (!), and are encouraged to continue enduring. Their joy in the midst of affliction would have resonated in a world where philosophical systems promised happiness in whatever the circumstances when one enjoys all that matters (e.g., Cicero, *Tusc.* 5.73; Diogenes Laertius, *Vit.* 10.118). As the Thessalonians imitate Paul and Jesus with joy amid persecution, should not modern believers imitate the Thessalonians?

"From you" (v. 8) is in an emphatic position. "Has sounded forth" could even be translated, with Chrysostom, as "roared" or "blasted" as the word (from/about the Lord) reaches wider and wider circles. Although Paul never *exhorted* his congregations to missionary labors, since that was his given task, he still expected them to be *involved* in those labors. Whether they themselves were evangelizing or the word had simply spread of their being evangelized, as they "turned toward God," their faith "toward God" expressed itself. On their *faith*, see the "believers" of v. 7, which influences how one should take "faith(fulness)" here.[17] Paul had no need to tell their story because along the Via Egnatia everyone already knew. They were "blasting" it! Verses 9–10 offer the content of what they were sharing.

Paul again describes in vv. 9–10 his "visit" (or "entrance") and reception at Thessalonica (1 Thess 1:5). "Visit" is used with an active sense in 2:1 immediately following. Apparently, the Thessalonians had been reporting that visit and its effect on their lives.[18]

Conversion is a "turning around" (Gal 4:9; 2 Cor 3:16), applied to the gentiles in the Jewish Scriptures (Ps 22:27 [21:28 LXX]; Isa 19:22; Jer 18:8), but even for Israel (Hos 5:4; 6:1; Joel 2:13). Jews would "turn" to join the Dead Sea community (e.g., CD XVI, 1–5). The gentile Thessalonians have turned from phony, dead idols to the living and true God—a Jewish, now early Christian claim (Jer 10:10; Jos. Asen. 11:10; Tertullian, *Res.* 24.1).

This living God will be returning in Christ, and the Thessalonians are to wait for that. Paul admonishes in this letter to live in a manner befitting the living Lord's arrival from the heavens (plural; also 2 Cor 12:2). He rescues "us" from the coming wrath (present in 1 Thess 2:16 and future in 5:9–10).[19] The coming wrath is *already* erupting into the present! Paul describes Christ as the deliverer from this wrath (also 2 Thess

---

17. With Kim and Bruce, *Thessalonians*, 182–83; contra Gupta, *Paul*, 80–85.
18. See Kim and Bruce, *Thessalonians*, 164–65.
19. Eschatological wrath against gentile vice and idolatry reflects a Jewish perspective on God's response to evil in the world (Sib. Or. 3.545–72; 5.75–89; 12.110–12).

1:6–10; Rom 11:26; Isa 59:20. The Thessalonians should not be surprised by this, since even the coming resurrection has erupted into the present with God's raising of Christ.

In a world replete with idolatrous cults, the Thessalonians had experienced a dramatic change. They had left paganism behind and with it their family, friends, communities, and customs. The new faith would be costly! Paul substitutes for the world they left behind a new community of brothers and sisters in Christ. One world has given way to another, and in due time everyone will be witness to it. Their Thessalonian neighbors would have been upset by their conversions. After all, Mount Olympus at ten thousand feet in elevation was visible fifty miles away![20] The gods would surely not treat this betrayal lightly. Even the emperor would be disappointed. Jesus as God's Son would be a challenge to imperial power. The emperor was regarded at Thessalonica as a son of the gods.[21] Coins minted in 27 BC celebrate on one side Julius Caesar as "god" and Augustus as his "son" on the other!

The Thessalonian Christ believers had been severed from their native social context, a situation foreign to most modern, Western Christians who appropriate this letter for themselves. The Thessalonians were alienated from their family, friends, and the surrounding world. The gospel had brought them into a *new* family under the Father, awaiting in hope their deliverance from the coming wrath. The Thessalonians had deconstructed their pagan, polytheistic way of viewing the world as represented by their parents, teachers, and friends, and were now incorporated into a new community. Paul's letter reinforces what they now "know" in this new (and distinct) community. Paul likewise challenges moderns to recognize their entry into the new world of the gospel.

Finally, the Pauline "gospel" differed significantly from the good news of Rome with its announcement of earthly peace and prosperity through its Savior, the emperor. Paul's gospel brought joy in the midst of persecution in the context of an invading, *new* reality. The Thessalonians had been adopted into a new family with implications for the resurrection from the dead and the final judgment. They were already enjoying that deliverance, even if its full impact was still to come. Continued persecution (3:3–4) is to be expected even for modern recipients of the letter. The Thessalonian Letters have therefore proven comforting for persecuted Christ believers through the centuries.

20. Mount Olympus 360° View.
21. *IG* X^2 I 31, 11.5–7, of Augustus.

2

1 Thessalonians 2:1–16

Paul and the Thessalonians' Experiences

Translation

[1] For you yourselves know, brothers and sisters, our visit to you, that it was not in vain, [2] but even though we had previously suffered and been insulted in Philippi, just as you know, we dared boldly with our God to speak to you the good news from God, amid considerable opposition. [3] For our appeal was not from error or from impure motives or from deceit, [4] but, just as we have been approved by God to be entrusted with the gospel, so we speak, not as those trying to please humans, but rather God, the one who tests our hearts. [5] For never once did we speak with flattering speech, just as you know, or with a greedy motive, as God is a witness, [6] nor seeking honor from people, neither from you nor from others [7] (even though we had the power to impose our authority as apostles of Christ), but we became infants in your midst. Just as a nurse cherishes her own children, [8] so, having tender affection for you, we were pleased to share with you not only the good news of God but also our very lives because you had become very dear to us.

[9] For you remember, brothers and sisters, our labor and toil, night and day; while working in order not to be a burden to any of you, we preached to you the good news from God. [10] You are witnesses and God also, how holy and righteous and blameless we were to you who

believed, [11] just as you know how [we treated] each one of you as a father his own children, [12] encouraging you and consoling and urging that you might walk worthily of God, who is calling you into his own kingdom and glory.

[13] And because of this indeed we ourselves continually give thanks to God because, when you received the word you heard from us of God, you received not a word of a human being but, just as it truly is—the word of God, which is indeed at work in you believers. [14] For you, brothers and sisters, became imitators of the assemblies of God in Judea in Christ Jesus, because you suffered the same things and you from your own fellow compatriots just as they also from the Jews [15] who killed both the Lord Jesus and the prophets and drove us out and do not please God and are hostile to all humanity [16] by hindering us from speaking to the gentiles so that they may be saved, with the result that they are always filling up the measure of their sins. Wrath has come upon them finally.

Commentary

In a narrative section running from 1 Thess 2:1 to 3:10, Paul reflects on his own and the Thessalonians' experiences, with frequent references to work, suffering, consolation, encouragement, and the word of the Lord. He reaffirms and reinforces the Thessalonians in what they already know, remember, and are doing. They are to stand firm on their current path.

Paul begins the chapter reviewing his style of preaching at Thessalonica (vv. 1–12) and closes focused on his converts (vv. 13–16). People—likely including the Thessalonians' own relatives, friends, coworkers, and neighbors—had questioned his preaching style and motivation (1 Thess 2:1–2). In response, he borrows from the stock description of an ideal philosopher, unlike the stereotypical wandering, street preacher with greedy, impure motives.[1] Paul's belaboring his own style of evangelism in 2:1–12 bears implications for the Thessalonians' approach. They are not to come across to pagan observers like the popular Sophists.[2] Paul

---

1. Note Dio Chrysostom's contrast of his own speech and teaching with those with false pretensions who really do not care (*Alex.* 32.11–12) (Malherbe, "Gentle" [1989]; Malherbe, *Letters to the Thessalonians*, 154).

2. Holtz, "Background," 78; but a point noted by commentators throughout the centuries, e.g., Olshausen in the late eighteenth and early nineteenth centuries (*Commentary*, 392).

therefore presents himself as the sort of *model* one finds in Greco-Roman moral exhortation as he contrasts his and his coworkers' preaching with that of the uneducated, popular street preachers and moralists of the Thessalonians' world.[3]

Paul and Silas had suffered in Philippi and were then opposed in their preaching of the gospel at Thessalonica (vv. 1–2).[4] Nevertheless, Paul's bold preaching was approved by God and did not spring from error or guile (vv. 3–4). He had not exercised his apostolic authority but chose instead to act in innocence (like infants) because of his care for them (vv. 5–8), as a father for his children (vv. 9–12).

The "for" in 1 Thess 2:1 links the narrative to 1:2–10, especially the reference to Paul's visit in 1:9 and how he had been an instrument of the gospel (1:5). Restating 1:5 from a negative standpoint, his visit to them was not "in vain."[5] Unlike the "empty" speech characteristic of popular rhetoricians with their displays of eloquence, Paul's ministry brought powerful results (also 3:5–6). The perfect tense behind what is here translated as "was" conveys the ongoing effects of the visit—indeed, what they already know and remember from that visit (2:2, 5, 9, 10, 11). First Thessalonians 2:1–12 is therefore building on 1:5–10, in which Paul's preaching (1:5) had led to the Thessalonians' renowned faith (1:6–8), with the powerful—even apocalyptic—effects of his visit further stated (1:9–10).

Paul narrates in v. 2 his suffering and humiliation and the "insults" he had endured at the Roman colony of Philippi before the difficult Thessalonica visit (which is described also in Acts 16:19–40; see also 2 Cor 11:23–29). At Thessalonica, too, he had experienced much opposition or contention (as what one would face in an athletic contest), but the gospel remains *of God* (2:13). *God* had raised Jesus from the dead (1:10) and was instrumental in bringing about Paul's preaching. God is mentioned nine times in 2:1–11 and Christ only once (in v. 7). Paul is openly, boldly preaching *God's* gospel. As John Calvin summarized the verse:

> The Thessalonians see that they had been called to faith not so much by a mere mortal as by God. . . .
>
> [Paul] proves this by two arguments. The first is that he had suffered persecution and indignity at Philippi. The second

---

3. Malherbe, "Exhortation" (1989); Malherbe, *Moral Exhortation*, 135–38.

4. Fee, *Thessalonians*, 55–56, 55n9, 59nn23–24.

5. See the eschatological vision of Isa 65:23; also Isa 49:4; Gal 1:15–17 (with its servant of the Lord allusions [Gal 2:2]).

is that a conflict of considerable proportions had developed at Thessalonica. We know that indignity and persecution weaken and indeed completely break men's minds. It was, therefore, a work of God that, although Paul had suffered various misfortunes and indignity, he appeared unaffected and did not hesitate to launch an assault on a large and wealthy city for the purpose of leading its people to Christ.[6]

Now ("for" [v. 3]) Paul explains *why* he had been so bold despite opposition. In vv. 3-6 he contrasts his exhortation—based on the comfort of the gospel—with that of other orators and philosophers. His exhortation does not stem from greed, praise seeking, trickery, deceit, flattery, or people pleasing—again, quite unlike that of the charlatan street preachers of the Greco-Roman world, who peddled a popular philosophy and lived off their recipients.[7]

Paul is an examined and approved agent of God (v. 4), entrusted with the gospel and not seeking to please human beings (see Gal 1:10). The people-pleasing charge survived him, even if based on his letters.[8] Rather, Paul is writing to please an audience of *One*, the One who tests and approves him—but also the Thessalonians (e.g., Jer 11:20)—the Lord, who examines hearts. John Wyclif remarked how some clergy are "infected by the splendour of the world and by avarice."[9] Similarly John Hus: false preachers seek monetary gain rather than integrity.[10] The seventeenth-century chaplain to King Charles I of England, Jeremy Taylor, warned against being desirous of human praise or being ashamed of one's trade or gainful employment.[11]

A series of negatives ensues in vv. 5-6 followed by a positive statement: Paul did not live off rhetorical performance or for selfish motives. He did not flatter his hearers ("How to Tell a Flatterer from a Friend," in Plutarch, *Mor.* 48E-74A) or preach from greed (Aristotle, *Eth. nic.* 4.6.9); note the false prophets of Jer 6:13; 8:10; Mic 3:5, 11. Paul calls God as his witness (Rom 1:9; Phil 1:8; 1 Thess 2:10; also Job 16:19). Flattery and greed characterize the charlatan street moralists. Quintilian, in the late first century, described orators shouting with their hands uplifted

---

6. Calvin, *Epistles*, 341.
7. So also Tertullian, *Pud.* 17.
8. *The Clementine Homilies* 18.10 (*ANF* 8:327) (Simon as a stand-in for Paul).
9. Wyclif, "On the Pastoral Office," 46.
10. Hus, "On Simony," 206.
11. Taylor, "Humility," 70-72 (ch. 2 secs. 4,1-6, 14); see 1 Thess 2:9-13.

and gesticulating for popular approval (*Inst.* 2.12.9). In a Mediterranean world of honor and shame, Paul is not seeking human honor or glory. Such conventions of praise—whether through monuments, inscriptions, philosophy, poetry, or even rhetoric—were all irrelevant. All that matters is relaying the good news God has sent.

Paul and his coworkers did not make financial demands of or "burden" the Thessalonians (v. 7), whether by asserting their apostolic authority or by touting their status. They did not insist on deferential treatment as apostles or "throw their weight around." Paul appeals, instead, to the imagery of a nurse or a nursing mother. "Her own children" suggests the latter (see Gal 4:19; Theocritus, *Id.* 27.66). Nurses, nevertheless, were widely recognized figures in the Greco-Roman landscape.[12] Similarly, Martin Luther avoided the status labels of "priest" or "cleric" in favor of "minister," "servant," or "steward," since serving others is at the heart of teaching the faith.[13]

The significantly stronger textual witness has *nēpioi* (children; note "orphaned" in 2:17) rather than *ēpioi* (gentle, and not a "burden," as in v. 7). If the first, then Paul is contrasting childlike innocence in his preaching with guile. He and his companions had become as lowly children in the Thessalonians' midst. Similarly in 1 Cor 14:20, he admonishes being "infants in evil" (i.e., in regard to evil).[14] An abrupt transition to "father" takes place in v. 11. The familial imagery, including—if original—the *nēpioi* (children or infants) of this verse, would bring to mind the labors of nurses. Augustine was so taken by the language of a nurse caring tenderly for her own children that he returned to it repeatedly in his writings. Also, Augustine described Paul, unlike arrogant monks, becoming small and refusing to employ flattery.[15] Origen viewed the humility and smallness of a child as the "perfect" model (*Comm. Matt.* 13.29 [*ANF* 10:492]).

On the other hand, ancient nurses were expected to be "gentle," a stock image for the genuine philosopher.[16] The extended contrast in

---

12. E.g., "How to Tell a Flatterer from a Friend," in Plutarch, *Mor.* 69 BC; Malherbe, "Gentle" (1989), 43–45.

13. Luther, "Freedom," 356.

14. "Innocent of the kind of skullduggery Paul is here dealing with" (Fee, *Thessalonians*, 71n62).

15. Augustine, *Op. mon.* 13.

16. Malherbe, "Gentle" (1989), 43, 43n53; Malherbe, *Letters to the Thessalonians*, 145–46; Soranus, *Peri Gynaikeion* 2.12 [32]; "How to Tell a Flatterer from a Friend," in Plutarch, *Mor.* 69.

1 Thess 2:1–12 between Paul's own preaching and that of the false street preachers favors this translation, and "gentle" would remove one of the abrupt transitions in imagery (in this case, from "infant" to "nurse").

Ultimately, "infants" is the more likely reading since it would explain a subsequent change in the manuscript tradition to "gentle" as a scribe sought to smooth the abrupt shifts in imagery (infant to nurse to father in v. 11; the latter shift is as abrupt as the first). In addition, the Greek letter *nu*—used at the end of the prior word and immediately again with "infants"—could have been accidentally omitted, resulting in *ēpioi* (gentle).[17]

"Her own" is more natural if in reference to a nursing *mother*; note the father in the following verses in the familial context of Thessalonian "brothers and sisters" (repeated in 1 Thess 2:1; 2:9). Chrysostom commented on vv. 7–8: "Nothing can be sweeter than such love."[18] Calvin noted how Paul's gentleness, as if a nurse, is reminiscent of a mother nursing her infant without dignity or power but sacrificing herself for the sake of the child's nourishment; thus was his affection and concern for the Thessalonians. A true pastor regards the church over his or her life.[19] A nurse caring for her very own children would not receive recompense for it—and neither does Paul (see Moses as a mother in Num 11:12).[20]

In agreement with the nurse image ("so"), Paul describes (v. 8) his tender, self-sacrificial affection for the Thessalonians while he had been in their midst.[21] His not "burdening" them agrees with the principles articulated in 1 Cor 4:12 (see Acts 18:3). Working as a craftsman "night and day" (from dawn to dusk, barely enough to survive) meant he had to preach in the cracks. He and his coworkers were sharing not only the gospel but their very selves, exemplifying the sacrificial nature of a true friend in antiquity, but even more so because of its Christ-likeness (e.g., Seneca, *Ep.* 9.10–11).

As evidence of his pure motives and care for them (in the previous verses), in v. 9 Paul reminds them how he had set an example by working with his hands. He will urge the Thessalonians to do the same later in 1 Thess 4:10b–12. His lifestyle defied any charge that he had sought

---

17. Conversely, the Greek letter *nu* ending the prior word could have been inadvertently repeated.
18. John Chrysostom, *Homilies on 1 Thessalonians* 2 (on 2:7–8) (NPNF[1] 13:330).
19. Calvin, *Epistles*, 344.
20. Gerber, *Paulus und seine "Kinder,"* 277–92, here 277.
21. Malherbe, *Letters to the Thessalonians*, 147.

money through ministry.[22] Paul embraces the demeaning hardships of manual labor; he refuses to be seen as a paid professional orator.[23] Sacrifice of self is at the heart of the gospel. He was likely sharing the gospel while working "night and day" (of necessity) in an impoverished world (1 Cor 4:12; 9:4-6, 14-15; 2 Cor 11:7-9).

Paul invokes his readers and even God as witnesses in vv. 10-12 of how he modeled proper behavior (unlike the charlatan): holy, righteous, and blameless toward both God and human beings. A verb must be filled in for v. 11's "just as you know how [I] ... each one of you, as a father with his children," whether "treated" or "exhorted." The maternal imagery in v. 7 has given way to the paternal. The apostle regularly describes himself elsewhere as a spiritual father to his churches, even as a Greco-Roman moral teacher would address disciples as children (1 Cor 4:15; 2 Cor 6:13; Phil 2:22; Phlm 10; 1 Tim 1:2).[24] Paul expresses tenderness and affection for his addressees in maternal terms, but instructions and advice in (caring) paternal terms.[25] God is calling the Thessalonians into his "kingdom" (fourteen times in Paul; e.g., Rom 14:17; 1 Cor 4:20), where they will enjoy *true* honor/glory (v. 12).

The new paragraph in v. 13 begins with another thanksgiving to God. On "the word you heard," see Rom 10:17. The Thessalonians received the preached word as it really was, the word of God. Historically, many have recognized this verse to be claiming the direct, divine inspiration of Paul's words.[26] Elsewhere, Paul explains that God's word creates faith (Rom 10:14-18); thus v. 13 here closes with the Thessalonians' belief. Augustine rightly attributed the Thessalonians' faith to God's gift-giving and empowering word.[27] The Lord enables their love to increase and abound.[28] Luther responded to those in his day who believed that the oral preaching of the word or the sacrament does not possess the power to save because they are mere externals: "I reply: There is a great difference between the external things of God and of man. God's external things are salvatory and efficacious. The poor people used to think that the external ministry of God was the same as the unfruitful traditions of

---

22. Jowett, *Epistles*, 1:55.
23. Thiselton, *Thessalonians*, 66.
24. Malherbe, *Letters to the Thessalonians*, 150.
25. Petersen, *Rediscovering Paul*, 128-31.
26. E.g., Ellicott, *Thessalonians*, 28.
27. Augustine, *Praed.* 39.
28. Augustine, *Grat.* 18.

the papists ... Satan has considered this, for it is his way to begin with the lowly things and eventually climb up to the heights."[29]

Verses 13–16 are authentically Pauline and build on the initial reference to persecution in 1 Thess 1:5–6.[30] The passage is not anti-Semitic but reflects God's judgment on the *persecuting* Jews, not *all* Jews (Rom 9–11). The Thessalonians have suffered the same sort of things from their own compatriots as the *Judean* Christ believers did from "the Jews." Their experiences thus mirror Paul's own at Philippi and in Thessalonica. Thessalonica was a hostile environment (1 Thess 1:6–10) where he faced great struggles (2:1–12), and the Thessalonians themselves have suffered (2:15–16). That suffering and struggle did not deter the Thessalonians from recognizing the word of God in Paul's preaching.

The emphatic "you" in v. 14 contrasts with the emphatic "we" in v. 3 (note "you" and "we" in 2:17). Verse 14 offers proof that the Thessalonians received Paul's message as *God's* word. The imitation motif from 1 Thess 1:6 reprises. The Thessalonians had become imitators of the Judean churches that had suffered persecution (in their case, coinciding with the rise of zealotism) but, in the case of the Thessalonians, most likely for adopting a strange, new, foreign *superstitio*, i.e., a disease afflicting the fabric of society. They are to imitate the churches in Judea, which are, ultimately, "in Christ Jesus" (as opposed to the ordinary Jewish assemblies). Paul identifies the plight of the Judean Christians likely because the gospel is "to the Jew *first*" (Rom 1:16). Paul singles out the persecuting Jews for censure precisely because of their priority in God's plan. Paul will affirm God's prioritization of the Jewish people in Rom 9–11.

Paul relays in vv. 15–16 a litany of evil with great emotion here. Verses 15–16 censure the Jewish leaders who rejected prophetic figures but, even more, Jesus himself. Still, Paul has in view *those responsible*. On the tradition of the Jews having killed their prophets, see 1 Kgs 18:4; 19:9–18; 2 Chr 24:19–21; Neh 9:26; Jer 2:20; 26:7–24; Mart. Isa. 5.1–14. The harsh response of other Jews to the prophets has now become a harsh response to Jewish Christ believers. Given his past as a persecutor, Paul would know exactly what he is saying. Even more, these Jews were now hindering Paul and the apostles from speaking to the gentiles so that they

---

29. Luther, "Katy Recommended," 318; citing Matt 10:20, Rom 1:16; 10:14; 1 Thess 2:13; 2 Thess 2:4.

30. For a fuller evaluation of the case against the Pauline authorship of these verses, see Das, *Paul and the Jews*, 128–39.

may be saved, preventing God's blessing and salvation from coming to all humanity (see Gen 12:3).

God's wrath has already come upon the persecutors "finally" or "until the end" (or "completion") (*eis telos*, paralleling *pantote*).[31] More likely, however, the aorist verb is proleptic, pointing to a future wrath, since by the early 50s none of the (local) actions taken against the Jews were of a level to fit God's wrath described as having already come upon the Jews.[32] The third-century Origen stressed that all people will face reward and punishment after the body is raised (*Princ.* pref. 5). The time of wrath is future in 1 Thess 1:10 and 5:9, and yet it has already erupted into the present! The Jews were hindering the preaching to gentiles (Isa 42:6; 49:6), and Paul relates this to the gentile Thessalonians (see their experiences in Acts 17:5–10, 13–14). Ironically, by preventing gentiles from being saved, the Jews themselves come under God's wrath.[33] The censure also serves a *social* function to demarcate the nascent Christ-believing movement as it defined itself.[34] For the early third-century Tertullian, Christ's followers must be prepared to suffer the same fate (*Marc.* 5.15.1). John Calvin described persecution as a special badge for Christ's soldiers.[35]

Perhaps most illustrative of potential anti-Semitic rhetoric is Martin Luther's infamous tractate *On the Jews and Their Lies*, and yet even in this work from his later years Luther emphasized that the persecution of 1 Thess 2:14–18 should not be blamed primarily on the Jews but rather on the activity of Satan.[36] In his earlier years, Luther had pointed to the hope for the Jewish people expressed in passages such as Rom 9–11, while stressing *God's miraculous work from within* rather than human efforts from without.[37] In his 1523 tractate *That Jesus Christ Was Born a Jew*, Luther referred to how the apostles, prophets, and patriarchs all came from the Jews, saying also: "I hope that if one deals in a kindly way with the Jews and instructs them carefully from the Holy Scripture, many of

---

31. Kim and Bruce, *Thessalonians*, 254.
32. Brookins, *Thessalonians*, 61–62.
33. Kim and Bruce, *Thessalonians*, 255.
34. Collins, "Vilification," 314.
35. Calvin, *Institutes* 3.8.7.
36. Luther, "On the Jews"; but Satan behind it all (e.g., 291).
37. In a letter to George Spalatin in January or February 1514, Luther wrote: "Conversion of the Jews will be the work of God alone operating from within, and not of man working—or rather playing—from without" ("Letter 6," 29).

them will become genuine Christians and turn again to the faith of their fathers, the prophets and patriarchs."[38] John Calvin appealed to Rom 11 to soften Paul's pronouncement here.[39] Calvin likewise recognized how Satan uses humans as his instrument for persecuting Christ's own.[40]

---

38. Luther, "That Jesus Christ," 200–201.
39. Calvin, *Epistles*, 349.
40. Calvin, *Epistles*, 350–51.

3

1 Thessalonians 2:17—3:13
Paul's Longing to See Them and News

Translation

[2:17] But as for us, brothers and sisters, although we have been orphaned from you for the time being—in person but not in heart—more than ever we were eager with much longing to see you face to face. [18] For this reason, we wanted to come to you—I, Paul, on more than one occasion—but Satan hindered us. [19] For who is our hope or joy or crown of boasting—is it not in fact you—before our Lord Jesus at his coming? [20] For you are our glory and joy.

[3:1] For this reason, because we were no longer able to bear it, we thought it best to be left alone in Athens, [2] and we sent Timothy, our brother and coworker of God in the gospel of Christ, in order to strengthen and encourage you regarding your faith, [3] so that no one would be disturbed by these afflictions. For you yourselves know that we were appointed for this. [4] In fact, when we were with you, we kept forewarning you, "We are to suffer affliction," as it has indeed happened, and [as] you know. [5] For this reason, when I myself could no longer endure it, I sent to find out about your faith, whether perhaps the tempter had tempted you and our labor had been in vain.

[6] But now Timothy has come to us from you and brought us good news about your faith and love and that you always have a fond

remembrance of us, longing to see us just as we also you—[7] for this reason we were consoled, brothers and sisters, because of you in all our distress and affliction, through your faith [8] because now we live if you yourselves are standing firm in the Lord. [9] For what thanksgiving can we to return to God concerning you for all the joy with which we rejoice because of you before our God, [10] begging night and day most earnestly in order to see your faces and to complete the things that are lacking in your faith?

[11] Now may our God and Father himself and our Lord Jesus make straight our way to you. [12] But as for you, may the Lord cause you to increase and abound in love for one another and for all, just as we also for you, [13] in order to establish your hearts as blameless in holiness before our God and Father at the coming of our Lord Jesus with all his holy ones. [Amen.]

Commentary

With "we" in 1 Thess 2:17, Paul turns from the Jews in the prior verses back to himself and his longing to see the Thessalonians. Paul and his coworkers are as children orphaned from their parents ("infants" in v. 7)—but only for the time being and not indefinitely.[1] He remains anxious and is striving to reestablish contact. As Thomas Aquinas commented, nothing is better than the presence of a friend.[2] Ultimately, Paul will be forced to send Timothy in his stead.

The "we" who wanted to come (v. 18) likely refers also to Silas and Timothy, but Satan prevented the visit (also Acts 16:7). From Paul's apocalyptic standpoint, hidden, spiritual forces are at work in the world with angels, demons, and Satan (1 Thess 2:19), along with a sequence of the ages: a present age followed by a day of wrath (5:1–2) and Christ's return (4:13–18). Later in 2 Thess 2:8–12, Paul will even identify a lawless one. Satan's efforts to stand in the way explain Paul's inability to visit, despite his intense desire to do so.

Paul wants desperately to visit them (vv. 19–20) since (*gar*) the Thessalonians are the crown (the laurel wreath for the victor) of his ministry, which he will lay at Jesus's feet (much as the Corinthians [1 Cor 9:2]). John Chrysostom in the fourth century commented on Paul's genuine

---

1. Weima, *Thessalonians*, 196–97.
2. Aquinas, *Commentary*, 21.

love and attachment to the Thessalonians.³ The Thessalonians are worthy of the boast in view of what God has done with them (also 1 Cor 3:10–15; 2 Cor 1:14; Phil 2:15; but not a human boast [1 Cor 1:29]): "Is it not in fact you?" The Thessalonians have given Paul *hope*, a key topic in the letter.⁴

"Coming" or "arrival" (*parousia*), a word long used for the visits of kings and emperors to their provinces, here is used for *Jesus* as the Lord who arrives; see the Tegea inscription of 192–93 CE: "In the year 69 of the first parusia of the god Hadrian in Greece."⁵ The Thessalonians are to be ready to welcome the true Lord at his coming (with the subtext: not Caesar). Calvin recognized that the Thessalonians would be revealed at the last day as Paul's joy and crown, when they too would enjoy glory and triumph. The apostle was urging his churches to act accordingly now in view of that future. They are to remain at the ready.⁶

With the opening "for this reason" in 1 Thess 3:1, Paul explains the actions he took when it had become clear that he could not visit the congregation. He had gotten to the point where he could no longer bear not knowing what was going on with the Thessalonians. His solution was to be left behind "alone" in Athens (also Acts 18:4–5). This may hint at a lack of success in the evangelization of Athens or, more likely given the context, having sent Timothy not long after having arrived in Athens. To be "left behind" suggests being bereft, emotionally (Aristotle, *Rhet.* 2.4.26; 3.16.5). "Thought it best" has been translated by some as "willingly," which would likewise suggest the sacrifice involved.⁷

Verse 5 replaces the "we" of v. 1 with an "I," indicating that Paul is the primary author of 1 Thessalonians and the team's leader.⁸ Silas was not a factor, then, in sending Timothy to Thessalonica, whether he remained behind with Paul or was at work elsewhere (Berea [Acts 17:10–11])—although he would be in agreement on the move (thus the "we").

Paul could have already been "alone" in Athens when he decided to send Timothy, who was at that point elsewhere. In either case, Paul would be left alone as a result. Casting a sideways glance, Acts 17:10–15

---

3. John Chrysostom, *Homilies on 1 Thessalonians* 3 (on 2:17) (*NPNF*¹ 13:334).
4. See the introduction; also 1 Thess 1:3; 5:8.
5. Deissmann, *Light*, 372; see also Bruce, *Thessalonians*, 57.
6. Calvin, *Epistles*, 351.
7. Best, *Thessalonians*, 130.
8. Neither quite a true plural nor an epistolary plural (Witherington, *Thessalonians*, 92n131).

1 THESSALONIANS 2:17—3:13

and 18:5 indicate that Timothy and Silas remained in Macedonia when Paul went on to Athens and rejoined him only in Corinth. Paul was delegating leadership to Timothy since the work was too much for one person alone. Paul's coworkers were essential.

Paul and his missionary group would form close relationships with strangers in a short time. God is made known in the context of personal relationships! Paul brings an incarnational perspective to his ministry labors.[9]

Timothy (v. 2) was the likely bearer of this letter. He might not have been as well known to the Thessalonians, thus requiring Paul's introduction as a "brother" and "coworker" (also Rom 16:3, 9, 21; Phil 2:25; 4:3; Phlm 24). He is *God's* coworker if one construes the genitive relationship as coworker *with* God—especially in view of the textual variants attempting to *remove* this sense—but Timothy could also be a coworker *for* God (similarly 1 Cor 3:9; 2 Cor 6:1).[10] The manuscript tradition evinces a concern with synergism in Paul's mention of God's coworker, but God is the primary actor in the evangelists' labors (1 Cor 3:5–13, esp. v. 9). Perhaps Paul and Timothy are working *alongside* their God in the spread of the gospel but, more likely, God is working *through* them (as in 2 Cor 5:18–20). Paul is indicating Timothy's high status in their movement.

Timothy is a coworker in the *gospel* of Christ, whether that gospel be *about* Christ or *from* Christ. He has been sent to strengthen the Thessalonians' faith in the face of the social pressures there. The need to "strengthen" and "encourage" their faith may be acute. His credentials are a reminder to heed his teaching.[11]

Paul's concern (v. 3) is that the trials or afflictions the Thessalonians were facing might disturb, shake, or upset them (see 1 Thess 1:6; 2:1–2).[12] Paul reminds them that they were destined for such suffering, as they already know (1 Thess 2:14; 5:9; 2 Thess 1:3–4). With John Chrysostom, "For not only ought we not grieve [about afflictions], but we ought even to rejoice in them. If you find consolation in forewarning, we tell you beforehand that here we have tribulation."[13] Christians outside the West can

---

9. Boring, *Thessalonians*, 121.
10. Wanamaker, *Thessalonians*, 128.
11. Kim and Bruce, *Thessalonians*, 275.
12. Malherbe, *Letters to the Thessalonians*, 192. For the papyri evidence for this sense, see Chadwick, "1 Thess 3³."
13. John Chrysostom, *Homilies on Ephesians* 7 (NPNF¹ 13:81).

attest to such severe, disturbing persecution (see the *Voice of the Martyrs* magazine and ministry).

Paul reminds the Thessalonians in v. 4 that, while with them, he had told them in advance that—directly quoting his earlier words—they should expect such suffering or persecution.[14] Now they have seen his words prove true (see also Acts 14:22). John Chrysostom commented:

> For greatly indeed, greatly does it tend to the comfort of others, to have heard from their teachers what is to happen. For as he that is sick, if he hear from his physician that this or that is taking place, is not much troubled; but if anything happens unexpectedly, as if he [the physician] too were at a loss, and the disorder was beyond his art, he is afflicted and troubled; so also is it here. Which Paul foreknowing, foretold to them, "we are about to be afflicted," "as it came to pass, and ye know." He not only says that this came to pass, but that he foretold many things, and they happened. "Hereunto we are appointed." So that not only ye ought not to be troubled and disturbed about the past, but not even about the future, if any such thing should happen, "for hereunto we are appointed."[15]

Those steeped in a tradition in which the faithful will always prosper will likely struggle with this expectation of suffering for Christian existence. As an apocalyptic thinker, Paul presents suffering as necessary for God's elect before the new age (fully) dawns (see Dan 12:1; 2 Bar. 70.2–10; 4 Ezra 5.1–13; 13.30–31; 14.16–17). John Calvin wrote: "Paul warns us that there is no reason for believers to entertain excessive fears in times of persecution, as though this were something strange or unprecedented. This is our condition, which the Lord has laid upon us."[16]

As Paul repeats in the singular in v. 5 what he had said in vv. 1–2, he adds that he was concerned that the tempter would take advantage of the Thessalonians' situation, leaving Paul's ministerial efforts there "in vain," a frequent concern in his letters (1 Cor 15:58; Gal 2:2; Phil 2:16; also LXX: Job 39:16; Isa 65:23). "Would be in vain" is in the subjunctive mood: a genuine possibility but not a reality (at least not yet).

Satan, the tempter, has sought to hinder Paul's ministry to the point that he is sincerely worried that the Thessalonians' faith would dissipate and his work end up being for nothing (also 1 Cor 7:5; 1 Thess 2:18). He

---

14. Malherbe, *Letters to the Thessalonians*, 194; Weima, *Thessalonians*, 214.
15. John Chrysostom, *Homilies on 1 Thessalonians* 3 (NPNF[1] 13:335).
16. Calvin, *Epistles*, 353.

wanted to check on ("know about") their faith. Paul's apocalyptic worldview is on display in these verses with the travails taking place before the end of this age with the dawning of the next and a hidden world in which Satan is active. Those afflicting the Thessalonians are effectively servants of Satan, and a realization of that fact would further encourage separation from the world into a new community.

With vv. 6–10 Paul relays how Timothy had arrived just prior to writing the letter. Timothy shared "good news." This is the only place in Paul's letters where the "good news" is not about Jesus (similarly Luke 1:19). "Gospel" is not a technical term for the early Christian message and could be used in Paul's day with reference to the emperor (note the Priene inscription celebrating the "good news" of Augustus's birth). Here the word bears the everyday sense of "good news" about the Thessalonians' faith and love. The Thessalonians even have "good" or fond memories of Paul's visit (also 1 Thess 1:5–9) and would love to see him.

Paul genuinely worries about the Thessalonians and is elated by good news from them. He is as committed to *strengthening* the faith of the Thessalonians as he was to convert them. Missionary labors and pastoral labors are not to be separated. Chrysostom noted: "You see [Paul's] anxiety in this matter, his regard for the good of his disciples, not less than for his own. For teachers ought to surpass natural parents, to be more zealous than they."[17]

The phrase "distress and affliction" in v. 7 reflects the influence of the same tandem in the Greek Septuagint (Job 15:24; Ps 24 [Eng./MT 25]:17; Zeph 1:15). The words refer to more than an internal state (Rom 5:3; 1 Cor 7:26–28; 2 Cor 1:8; 6:4; 12:10; 1 Thess 1:6; 3:3). The two words are in the context of physical deprivation and violence in 2 Cor 6:4–5. Paul has used the *thlib-* root three times so far in 1 Thess 3: for the Thessalonians' afflictions (v. 3), for what awaits Christ believers (v. 4), and here for Paul's own afflictions. Paul is thereby *identifying with* the Thessalonians in what they are experiencing.[18]

Thanks to the "good news" buoying Paul's mood (v. 8), "now we live." The good news likely motivated Paul to write 1 Thessalonians. Calvin noted how *all* pastors' moods are affected by the situation of their churches, whether they experience happiness or grief.[19]

---

17. John Chrysostom, *Homilies on 2 Timothy* 2 (NPNF[1] 13:481).
18. Brookins, *Thessalonians*, 74.
19. Calvin, *Epistles*, 354–55.

"If you yourselves are standing firm" is a conditional clause that assumes that the Thessalonians may not stand firm, but the indicative verb encourages them to.[20] Faith may grow, or it may shrink away. Paul would not agree with the "once saved, always saved" slogan. He regularly encourages his congregations to grow in their faith by the grace and power of God. The highest cluster of faith references in the letter is in 1 Thess 3:2–10. They are to stand firm in the Lord (3:7–8) since Jesus died and rose again (4:14). Faith in God (1:8–10) includes also faith in Christ, and Paul must encourage them in this faith. Faith and love accompany each other (1:3; 3:6; 5:8). Faith must lead to loving works on behalf of others as Paul models that other-centeredness in his concern for the Thessalonians. This reciprocal love within the community of faith should also abound "for all" (3:11; 5:15).

Paul realizes in vv. 9–10 that he can never thank God enough. He expresses a desperate desire to see the Thessalonians again, praying "night and day" for this in order to supply what is lacking in their faith. Prayer at night suggests a deep concern (Pss 42:8; 63:6; 77:2; 2 Macc 13:10; 1QS VI, 6–8). What is lacking in their faith (but not entirely absent!) is suggested by the triad at the beginning and near the end of the letter (faith, love, and hope [1 Thess 1:3; 5:8]): hope. Why that should be the case will be clear in the next chapter of the letter with the situation of loved ones who have died. Nevertheless, their faith and love *are* "good news." Paul *praises* their hope in 1:3, even as there is something lacking in their *faith* (3:10). What is lacking, then, is an even *greater* hope. He wants to "complete" what they are lacking.

"For all the joy with which we rejoice" (also 1 Thess 2:19–20) contrasts with "in all our distress and affliction" in v. 7.[21] Paul still relies on and finds encouraging—even to the point of rejoicing—the report of their faith (v. 7). What specifically they are lacking refers to *several* concerns and *not just* greater hope, as identified in 4:1—5:22: including the fate of those in their community who have died, sexual holiness, and love within the community of faith.[22]

The Thessalonians were acting as those who have no hope (1 Thess 4:13). In 1:3 Paul describes the *endurance* of hope in developing pairings from his initial triad of faith, *endurance*, and love—especially in his

---

20. Fee, *Thessalonians*, 125; Weima, *Thessalonians*, 224–25.

21. For the fuller pattern of parallels between vv. 7 and 9 (because of you/about you; through your faith/on your account), see Kim and Bruce, *Thessalonians*, 291.

22. Weima, *Thessalonians*, 228–29.

second letter: faith and love (2 Thess 1:3), endurance and faith (2 Thess 1:4), love and endurance (2 Thess 3:5). Faith and love are a regular combination for Paul (1 Cor 16:13–14; 2 Cor 8:7; 2 Thess 1:3; Phlm 5).[23]

Having talked about how he prays for them night and day, even better, Paul breaks off into a prayer for them in vv. 11–13. William Law in the eighteenth century was impressed by Paul's devoted prayer life on behalf of his congregations, even as a father would constantly pray for his own children.[24] With these verses, Paul is inviting the Thessalonians to join in that prayer before God, even as he admonishes them. Note also that the Christian life is lived in freedom. Paul *admonishes* them. He persuades rather than dictates.

The prayer in vv. 11–13 is transitional, recapping what came before and paving the way for the exhortations in chs. 4–5. The recap includes: (1) the Thessalonians' love (1 Thess 1:3; 3:6, 12); (2) the reciprocal love between the Thessalonians and Paul (3:6, 12); (3) Paul's desire to see them (2:17–18; 3:12); and (4) Christ's coming (1:10; 2:19; 3:13). The prayer anticipates: (1) love (3:12; 4:9–10); (2) sanctification/holiness (3:13; 4:3–4, 7; 5:23); and (3) Christ's coming (3:13; 5:1–11, 23).[25]

The prayer is also to the Lord Jesus and not just God the Father as in a Jewish prayer. In the Jewish Scriptures *Yahweh* is "Lord" (e.g., Deut 6:4; see 1 Cor 8:6). Here Jesus is "Lord." At the same time, both God the Father and the Lord Jesus are identified as Paul employs a singular verb for the plural subject—although the point cannot be pressed too hard.[26] Paul, at this early point in the Christ movement, held an unusually high Christology with no sense that it was a novelty or an innovation. Paul simply could not think of God apart from Christ. In fact, the names are reversed in 2 Thess 2:16–17. Early Christian authors noted the high Christology here as well.[27] God is both the Father and the Lord Jesus, with Ambrose of Milan: "Again, that thou mayest know that the Father is, and the Son is, and that the work of the Father and the Son is one. . . . Both Father and Son are named, but there is unity of direction, because

---

23. Brookins, *Thessalonians*, 74–75.
24. Law, *Serious Call*, 291, 301.
25. Malherbe, *Letters to the Thessalonians*, 211; Brookins, *Thessalonians*, 78.
26. Bruce and Brookins note the similar construction with the singular verb for "heaven and earth" in Matt 5:18; "the wind and the sea" in Mark 4:41; and "gold and silver" in Jas 5:3 (Bruce, *Thessalonians*, 71; Brookins, *Thessalonians*, 77).
27. E.g., Theodoret of Cyrus, *Letter* 146 ($NPNF^2$ 3:316–23).

unity of power."²⁸ Matthew Poole in the seventeenth century noted how Christ is the object here of divine worship.²⁹ The Father and the Lord Jesus are able to bring about what Paul requests (also Num 6:24–26; Ps 20:1–5; 2 Macc 1:2–6). Jesus is determining Paul's actions and itinerary here and not just God the Father (as elsewhere; Rom 1:10; 15:32; see the undefined "Lord" in 1 Cor 4:19; 16:7).³⁰

Right after also mentioning God the Father, in v. 12 Paul prays *just* to the Lord (Jesus). Paul limits his prayer to Christ the Lord elsewhere only in 2 Cor 12:7–9. The prayer to increase and abound in love prepares for 1 Thess 4:9–12 and recalls the Thessalonians' love for Paul in 3:6–10. God will give them a greater and greater capacity to love each other, just as that same love binds Paul to them. Love and holiness are both essential and to be encouraged. Paul wants their love for each other to overflow. When he refers to their love "for all," this is not likely "all believers" beyond Thessalonica since Paul would have clarified that, as he does elsewhere (e.g., 1 Cor 7:17; 14:33). Likely Paul has in mind "all" with whom the Thessalonians are in contact, including unbelievers, a challenging request in view of the afflictions they are enduring.³¹ Paul has already set an example in his love for them.

Verse 13 forms an *inclusio* with 1:3, thereby framing chs. 1–3. "In order to" in v. 13 parallels v. 2. Paul concludes his prayer for the Thessalonians by stressing the need to be holy in view of Jesus's impending return with the holy ones, a holiness he further encourages in 1 Thess 4:1–12, even as 4:13—5:11 addresses what happens to the dead in Christ when Jesus comes with his holy ones. The goal is for the Thessalonians to be found blameless in holiness before God at Christ's coming, as is to be expected for God's people—thus also God's requirement for Israel (Exod 19:6; Lev 11:44; Deut 26:19). Those meeting Christ upon his return will be as holy as those coming from heaven with Christ. The Thessalonians will be holy as *God* is holy (Pss 71:22; 89:18; Isa 1:4; Ezek 39:7). Paul will shortly return to God's will for them to be holy in 4:3.

In this liturgical formulation, those accompanying Christ from heaven are most likely angels and not the saints (see 2 Thess 1:7, 10; Ps 89:5; Dan 4:10–13; 1 En. 1.9; 1QH XI [=III], 22; IV, 25; 1QM III, 2–5; Matt 13:41; Mark 8:38; 13:27; Jude 14). The saints will reunite with Jesus

---

28. Ambrose, *Of the Christian Faith* 2.10.87 (*NPNF*² 10:235).
29. Poole, *Commentary*, 3:741.
30. Furnish, *Thessalonians*, 83.
31. Furnish, *Thessalonians*, 84; also 1 Thess 5:15.

when he comes and not before (1 Thess 4:15–18). This is the language used to describe the "day of the Lord" (e.g., Zech 14:5) now applied to Christ. Matthew 25:31 draws on the same Zechariah text but changes "holy ones" to "angels." In these texts God's appearance and the subsequent judgment will take place on *earth* (Pss 50:3; 68:1–7; 80:1; 82:8; Isa 26:19; 42:13; 63:9; 64:1; 66:18; Dan 7:13–14; Zeph 1:5; Mal 4:1).

On the other hand, a case can be made for "saints" accompanying Christ rather than the angels since every other Pauline instance of the word refers to Christ believers (Rom 1:7; 8:27; 12:13; 15:25; 1 Cor 1:2; 6:1–2; 2 Cor 1:1; Phil 1:1; 4:22). Further, 2 Thess 1:7 uses the word "angels" instead, with "holy ones" in 2 Thess 1:10 referring to the saints who believed. If "holy ones" in 3:13 is referring to believers, then Paul would be anticipating the holiness required of the congregation in advance of Christ's return in 1 Thess 4:3–8, 13–18. Once believers join Christ in the air, they will escort him back to earth in 1 Thess 4:17 and thus will be *with him* at his coming.[32] (Paul offers no indication in v. 13 that he is referring to *pre-raptured* saints. Dispensationalism runs aground on this letter.) Arguably, the appeal to Zechariah to take the word as "angels" is not as helpful as an approach based on the context of the letter: what Paul expects the *Thessalonians* to be gleaning in view of Christ's impending return. Finally, Paul is often rather negative about angels in his letters; e.g., powers potentially separating believers from Christ (Rom 8:38); entities judged by believers at the last day (1 Cor 6:3); Satan's disguising himself as an angel (2 Cor 11:14); Satan's own angels (2 Cor 12:7); and mediators of the problematic law (Gal 3:19).[33]

"In holiness *before* our God and Father at the coming of our Lord" conveys that the Thessalonians will be in the very presence of God at *the same time* that Jesus returns. God and Christ will therefore judge together. The God who judges is the same God who has revealed himself in Jesus.[34] The coming of the Lord with all the holy ones (angels) in Zech 14:5 has now become the coming of the Lord Jesus.[35]

---

32. Weima, *Thessalonians*, 242–43. For Kim and Bruce, it complicates v. 13 to imagine believers rising up into the air only to accompany Christ back down (*Thessalonians*, 303), but Weima and others are relying on a Greco-Roman commonplace in greeting an arriving dignitary.

33. Boring, *Thessalonians*, 127–28.

34. Witherington, *Thessalonians*, 104.

35. Fee, *Thessalonians*, 134.

4

1 Thessalonians 4:1–12
Exhortation

Translation

[1] As for other matters, then, brothers and sisters, we ask and exhort you in the Lord Jesus that—just as you received from us how it is necessary for you to walk and so to please God, just as you are in fact walking—you would do so more and more. [2] For you know what commands we gave you through the Lord Jesus. [3] For this is God's will, your holiness: that you keep away from sexual sin, [4] that each of you know how to control his own vessel in holiness and honor, [5] not in the passion of sexual desire as the gentiles, who do not know God, [6] in order not to trespass against and defraud his brother in this matter, because the Lord is an avenger of justice concerning these things, just as also we forewarned you and testified. [7] For God did not call us to impurity but in holiness. [8] Consequently, the one who rejects [this] is not rejecting a human being but God, who indeed gives his Holy Spirit into you.

[9] Now about brotherly love, you have no need [for us] to write you, for you yourselves are taught by God to love one another. [10] For indeed you are doing it to all the brothers and sisters in the whole of Macedonia. Yet we are exhorting you, brothers and sisters, to do so more and more, [11] and to make it your ambition to live quietly and to mind your own affairs and to work with your [own] hands, just as we also commanded

you, [12] in order that you may walk becomingly in the eyes of outsiders and that you might have need of no one.

Commentary

In a major shift ("as for other matters"), Paul turns to what was lacking in the Thessalonians' faith (1 Thess 3:10) in a section devoted to exhortation, concerns typically placed toward the end of Paul's letters: sexual holiness (4:1-8), brotherly love and work (4:9-12), those in Christ who have died (4:13-18), Christ's return for believers still living (5:1-11), leaders of the community, and living at peace with neighbors (5:12-15). In an *inclusio* binding vv. 1-11 together, one should walk/live "just as we also commanded you" (v. 11), matching v. 1's "you received from us how it is necessary for you to walk."[1] The connection between religion and ethics reflects the Jewish roots of the Christ faith (otherwise unusual in the Greco-Roman world).[2] Apocalyptic and eschatological concerns continue to dominate as Paul reminds his hearers where they live in history.

"As for other matters" (v. 1) marks a new section as Paul begins his exhortations (translating it "finally" would be inappropriate [e.g., Phil 3:1, unlike Phil 4:8]). "Ask" and "exhort" emphasize the request.[3] Drawing on an appeal formula from ancient letters, Paul reminds them that they have already received his apostolic instruction on these topics and should continue on their current path "more and more" (*perisseuēte mallon* [vv. 1, 10]). They are living as "is necessary" for them "to walk" "to please God," leaving a way of life and thinking behind. Paul expects holiness in their personal relations. Paul had commanded (*parangelias* [v. 2]) as "in the Lord Jesus," with the Lord's authority as the congregation's founder.

The holiness Paul identifies as God's will in v. 3 is moral and not ritual. Avoidance of sexual sin will allow the Thessalonians to be "blameless in holiness" at the Lord's coming (1 Thess 3:13).[4] The sexual sin of *porneia* includes extramarital and premarital relations. Note the presence in the original of the article, signaling a generic quality.[5] In a world of

1. Fee, *Thessalonians*, 162.
2. Boring, *Thessalonians*, 135.
3. Kim and Bruce, *Thessalonians*, 322.
4. Paul's call to holiness would figure among the eighteenth-century Pietists, e.g., Oetinger (*Wörterbuch*, 313-14).
5. Das, *Remarriage*, 114-41.

mistresses and concubines, Paul exhorts the Thessalonians to a countercultural holiness (unlike Demosthenes, [*Neaer.*] 59.122; Horace, *Sat.* 1.2.31–35; Cicero, *Cael.* 20.48; Plutarch, *Conj. praec.* 144F). The Thessalonian Cabirus and Dionysus cults ritualized *porneia*, with prominent displays of the phallus; note 4:4's "vessel." The cults placated gods with rituals, but rarely moral requirements. The Christ believers, like Israel, are to be holy and sanctified to God (Lev 11:44–45; 19:2; 21:8). Such behavior conforming to God's own holiness will distinguish them, often requiring separation or abstention. Martin Luther brought this verse and Heb 12:14 into relation since holiness will be necessary to see the Lord.[6] Paul could be reinforcing in this letter the apostolic decree of Acts 15:20, 22, 27, 29 (note Silvanus's role in Acts 15).[7]

Paul uses the word "vessel" (*skeuos*) in vv. 4–5 figuratively (as in Rom 9:21–23; 2 Cor 4:7). The word could refer either to a wife or to one's own body/member. The majority interpret Paul's contrast as between those who know God with their self-control vs. gentiles with their passionate desires, but the decision between the two options is difficult, as the history of interpretation shows.

Favoring a reference to a *wife* rather than to the body or male genitalia (i.e., gaining control over one's desires or body):[8]

1. If referring to the body, one would need to translate the verb *ktasthai* with the unattested sense of "to acquire mastery/control over." Translated more naturally as "acquire" or "gain possession of" would make little sense for one's own body.[9] On the other hand, the Hebrew *bāʿal* is used for "buy/acquire" as well as to "have control of." To purchase is to *gain control* over. Perhaps Paul's use of the Greek *ktasthai* reflects the Hebrew parallel.

2. Paul uses other euphemisms for the male genitalia (e.g., 1 Cor 12:23–24), where those parts are plural, but here *skeuos* is singular. On the other hand, 1 Cor 12 is a discussion of the "body" (*sōma*),

---

6. Luther, "Epistle to the Hebrews," 235.

7. Witherington, *Thessalonians*, 112, following Lightfoot; also Kim and Bruce, *Thessalonians*, 331.

8. *Wife* with, e.g., Basil the Great, *Letter* 160.5 (*NPNF*[2] 8:214); Jerome, *Letter* 128.3 (*NPNF*[2] 6:259); Theodore of Mopsuestia, *Commentaries*, 466–67; Augustine, *Nupt.* 9[8]; Augustine, *Serm.* 1.21; Aquinas, *Commentary*, 30; Luther, "Lectures on 1 Timothy."

9. So stresses the nineteenth-century Lünemann (*Handbook*, 108–9).

requiring that language. The physical body is a key element in Paul's thinking in Rom 12:1 and 1 Cor 6:12–20.

3. The adjective "his own" contrasts with someone else's.

4. Honor was a regular *topos* in Greco-Roman discussions for what was due a marital partner (Xenophon, *Hier.* 3.4; Plutarch, *Conj. praec.* 143B). To maintain that honor, sexual relations are to be confined to one's spouse (1 Cor 7:1–7).

5. *Ktasthai* could bear an ingressive sense: "acquiring," "taking possession of" a wife. If durative, Paul is talking about holy conduct within marital life.

Favoring a reference to *body* rather than wife:[10]

1. How would one acquire his *own* wife (she is already his) or "know how" to *acquire* a wife?[11]

2. David's men in 1 Sam 21:5 avoided sexual relations so that their "vessels" (bodies) would be consecrated to God.

3. Instructions for mastery over one's own body would apply to women as well.[12] Paul is addressing the *entire* Christ-believing community and not just the married.

4. Paul does not mention "wives" in this more general context ("*each of you*"). He does not use the phrase "take *a wife*" (*ktasthai gynaika*) as in Sir 36:24 LXX; Ruth 4:5. "Your own" as a warning against acquiring *other* men's wives would be out of place.[13]

5. A wife is a "vessel" in 1 Pet 3:7, but *so also* is a husband (the "weaker" entails a stronger).[14]

6. "Each of you" would impose a marital *requirement*, contrary to Paul's advice to remain single, if possible (1 Cor 7).[15]

---

10. *Body* with Tertullian, *Res.* 16; Ambrosiaster, *Commentaries*, 107; Souter, *Pelagius' Expositions*, 429; Theodoret of Cyrus, *Commentaries*, 2:115 (stressing that the instructions are for *all* believers); Calvin, *Epistles*, 359 (explaining that "wife" is too forced in this context); Bengel, *Word Studies* 2.482; Olshausen, *Commentary*, 429–30.

11. Smith, "1 Thessalonians 4:4."

12. Wanamaker, *Thessalonians*, 153.

13. Fee, *Thessalonians*, 147–48.

14. Wanamaker, *Thessalonians*, 152.

15. Fee, *Thessalonians*, 147–48.

7. "Vessel" means "body" in 2 Cor 4:7, as also in Jewish ethics.[16] In addition, the *body* is the Spirit's temple in 1 Cor 6:19. On dishonoring the body, see also Rom 1:24–27; 12:1.

8. "Acquiring a wife in passionate lust" is anachronistic since in the first-century world wives were "acquired" for household management and procreation.[17]

In short, one should know how to gain control over (an ingressive sense) one's own vessel.[18] Gentiles express those desires in ways that are contrary to those who know God.

In a potential both-and approach, Paul could be faulting passionate, lustful gentiles for enjoying sexual relations apart from the marital union.[19] The sexual organ used with "passionate lust" defrauds someone. Such instructions require a departure from a world where sex was readily available with slaves and prostitutes.

Ambrose of Milan warned "not to enkindle the fires of passion . . . in every season. . . . Let there be no immorality and uncleanness in the servants of God, because we are servants of the unspotted Son of God. Let each one know himself and possess his vessel, and when the soil of the body has been ploughed, let him wait for the fruit in due season . . . and in the once thickly wooded frailty of passion let there flourish ingrafted virtues."[20]

Chrysostom at times favored taking "vessel" as a person's body: "It is, then, a matter to be learnt, and that diligently, not to be wanton. But we possess our vessel, when it is pure; when it is impure, sin possesses it. . . . Here he shows also the manner, according to which one ought to be temperate; that we should cut off the passions and lust."[21] He also seems to take the word here as a reference to one's spouse: "For we grieve not so much, when our riches are carried off, as when marriage is invaded. . . . So that even if thou shouldest defile the Empress, he says, or even thine own handmaid, that hath a husband, the crime is the same."[22]

---

16. Thiselton, *Thessalonians*, 97.
17. Fee, *Thessalonians*, 147–48.
18. Smith, "1 Thessalonians 4:4," 84–85.
19. For such both-and positions in history, see, e.g., the seventeenth-century Matthew Poole, leaning toward "body" (*Commentary*, 3:742).
20. Letter 15, from Ambrose to Constantius (AD 379), in Ambrose, *Letters*, 79.
21. John Chrysostom, *Homilies on 1 Thessalonians* 5 (NPNF¹ 13:344).
22. John Chrysostom, *Homilies on 1 Thessalonians* 5 (NPNF¹ 13:345).

Pagans are immoral and do not know God, a common Jewish assertion (Job 18:21; Ps 79:6 [78:6 LXX]; Jer 10:35; Wis 14:12–27; Sib. Or. 3.29–45; T. Naph. 3.2–5; 4.1). For Paul, passions and desires guide pagan actions (Rom 1:29–31; 2:21–22; 13:13; 1 Cor 5:9–11; 6:9–10; 2 Cor 12:20–21; Gal 5:19–21). He contrasts the audience with pagans since at least most of them were not Jews.[23] The popular Cabirus and Dionysus cults both included orgiastic practices that would not be tolerated in the Thessalonian Christ-believing assembly. If they are no longer like the gentiles and are not Jews, then they are, effectively, a *third* group within humanity.[24]

The verb *pleonektō* in v. 6 normally means "defraud" (e.g., Dio Chrysostom, *Avar.* 17.8). A reference to commercial language (business ethics) is abrupt when v. 7 seems to refer again to sexual aberrations.[25] "In *this* matter" refers back to the sexual immorality introduced in v. 3. Verses 3–6 are a single sentence, and the mention of holiness in v. 7 signals that the topic remains sexual behavior. Marriages were usually arranged and viewed as property transactions. To invade a marriage was to defraud a husband of his property rights.[26] Alternatively, Paul could be using the verb with the sense of "act covetously toward the brother"; note the noun *pleonexia* in 1 Thess 2:5.[27]

Drawing on apocalyptic language, the Lord will avenge the evil, a common OT motif (esp. Ps 94:1; but also Exod 7:4; 12:12; Deut 32:35; Ps 18:47; Jer 11:20; Mic 5:15; T. Reu. 6.6; T. Jos. 20.1; T. Benj. 10.8–10; 2 Thess 1:8)—something Paul stresses he has already forewarned them. The title "Avenger" is placed at the beginning of the clause in order to give it emphasis in the Greek.

In v. 7 believers were not called to a life of (sexual) debauchery or impurity but to a state of holiness by a holy God. They are sanctified by God (similarly 2 Thess 2:13–14). Note the *inclusio* with sexual holiness in v. 3, framing the subunit. To reject this teaching (v. 8) is to reject God's will and his gift of the Holy Spirit (stress "holy" in this context; see 2 Thess 2:13). The Thessalonians were likely struggling to live in this countercultural manner, but God "gives" what they need, the Holy Spirit (see Ezek

---

23. Witherington, *Thessalonians*, 116.
24. Wanamaker, *Thessalonians*, 154.
25. Wanamaker, *Thessalonians*, 154.
26. The nineteenth-century Denney, *Thessalonians*, 142; also Malherbe, *Moral Exhortation*, 153.
27. Witherington, *Thessalonians*, 117.

37:6, 14). Note the verbal parallels in this verse to Ezek 36:25–27 (holiness, cleansed from impurity/uncleanness, idols, giving the Spirit). This holy life, through the Spirit, is the fulfillment of Ezekiel's prophecy.

Having addressed how *not* to relate to the brothers and sisters, Paul turns to brotherly love in vv. 9–12 with the transitional "now about" flagging a new topic—whether they had asked him about this or not (e.g., 1 Cor 7:1, 25). Verse 9 forms an *inclusio* with v. 12 with the word "need." When Paul complements them, saying he does not need to write them, one may well ask why then was he writing? Paul will turn to that primary rationale shortly (in vv. 13–18); also 2 Cor 9:1; 1 Thess 5:1; Phlm 19.

Non-Christ believers regularly used *philadelphia* for love between blood relations. Here brotherly love is to be toward those *in Christ* (likewise Rom 12:10; Heb 13:1; 1 Pet 1:22; 2 Pet 1:7)—another instance of the intimate family language of the letter. Rejected by friends and relatives for their strange, new faith, they enjoy a *new* family.

The Thessalonians are "God taught" (similarly John 6:45; Barn. 21.6) in what may be the first use of this Greek word, which likely alludes to Isa 54:13 where "all your sons will be taught by God," or perhaps Lev 19:18's command to love the neighbor (thus Thomas Aquinas) (also Jer 31:33–34; Ezek 26–27; 1 Cor 2:13).[28] They have been taught by God how to love and are enabled by his Spirit.

They are to continue doing so (loving each other) in *all* of Macedonia (v. 10; 2 Cor 8:1–2). Paul had built up a social network of mutual support and financial aid (e.g., Phil 4:14–18). "To do so" (or "abound") is the first of four or five subordinate infinitives dependent on "we exhort/appeal." Those who are idle (mentioned in 5:14) are *disrupting* that brotherly love.

Having addressed the Thessalonians' relationships among themselves (v. 9) and with fellow Christians in the region (v. 10), Paul turns in vv. 11–12 to their relationships with outsiders. *Philotimeisthai* (make it your ambition) was used in political or philanthropic contexts for achieving a political end by benefaction while seeking honor or distinction ("On the Tranquility of Mind," in Plutarch, *Mor.* 465F–466A). By Paul's day, it meant to "aspire" or "earnestly endeavor" (Rom 15:20; 2 Cor 5:9). In an oxymoron and counterintuitively: make it your ambition to live quietly.[29] Christ believers are *not* to seek prestige or public status but to

---

28. Fee, *Thessalonians*, 160; Aquinas, *Commentary*, 32.
29. Bengel, *Word Studies* 2.483; Brookins, *Thessalonians*, 90.

live in a "quiet" way. (A low profile would be helpful amid persecution.) Paul has, however, *praised* their evangelistic efforts (1 Thess 1:7–8).[30]

They are to mind their own business and work hard, even with their hands (also 2 Thess 3:12), fulfilling the expectation of Greco-Roman moralists to avoid dependencies or taking advantage of people (e.g., Dio Chrysostom, *Ven.* 7.103–153). The question is not, then, who is to be dependent on the church's aid, but rather how Christians express love toward others (Rom 13:8; see also Luke 10:25–37).[31] Outsiders will be watching with a critical eye, and thus Christian behavior is to be "becoming" (the same word in Rom 1:27; 13:13; 1 Cor 7:36; 14:40; Dio Chrysostom, *Ven.* 7.110–125).

Paul espouses a healthy work ethic (Gen 3:17–19; Job 1:10; Prov 10:4; Eph 4:28) and sets an example (1 Thess 2:9; 2 Thess 3:8; also Acts 20:33–34; 1 Cor 4:12). With John Calvin, "There is nothing more disgraceful than an idle good-for-nothing who is of no use either to himself or to others. Nothing is more unseemly than someone who is idle and good for nothing; they profit neither themselves nor others, and seem to have been born merely to eat and drink."[32]

---

30. Kim and Bruce, *Thessalonians*, 365; contra Barclay, "Conflict," 520–25. This is about those who stopped working in view of Christ's imminent coming (1:9–10; 4:13—5:11; 2 Thess 3:6–15)—and thus leading naturally into how they were living off others' generosity in the church, thereby disrupting it.

31. Brookins, *Thessalonians*, 91–92; Malherbe, *Letters to the Thessalonians*, 256.

32. Calvin, *Epistles*, 362.

5

1 Thessalonians 4:13–18
The Fate of Those in Christ Who Died

Translation

[13] BUT WE DO not want you to be ignorant, brothers and sisters, about those who are asleep so that you do not grieve like the rest who have no hope. [14] For if we believe that Jesus died and arose, so also God will bring with him, through Jesus, those who have fallen asleep. [15] For this we say to you by the word of the Lord that we who are alive who are left until the coming of the Lord will by no means have an advantage over those who have fallen asleep, [16] because the Lord himself, with a loud summons, with the voice of the archangel, and with the trumpet of God, will descend from heaven, and the dead in Christ will rise first; [17] then we who are alive who are left will be caught up in clouds together with them to meet the Lord in the air, and so we will always be with the Lord. [18] So then, comfort one another with these words.

Commentary

Paul introduces a new topic in v. 13 by saying he did not want the Thessalonians to be ignorant (similarly Rom 11:25; 1 Cor 10:1; 12:1). This is the *only* so-signaled first-time instruction in a letter full of reminders of what

1 THESSALONIANS 4:13–18

they already know and do not need written to them (1 Thess 5:1–2; also 2:11–12; 3:3–4; 4:2, 6, 9, 11). Nothing suggests that the Thessalonians would dissent from or doubt any of this new teaching. "So then" in v. 18 signals the conclusion of the paragraph.

Sleep is a euphemism for death. Some in the Thessalonian congregation have clearly died before Christ's return. Note: Paul does not celebrate any Christlike martyrdoms or near-martyrdoms as the cause of that sleep (also Rom 16:4; Phil 2:25–30). The present tense of the participle for "those falling asleep" may allow application not only to those already dead but also those who *will* die before Christ's coming.

The idea of the "sleeping" being raised in body is not likely a novel idea for the Thessalonians, as if Paul had never suggested it, but likely reflects difficulty in grasping the concept (similarly Acts 17:18–20, 31–32; 26:6–8; 1 Cor 15:12, 35).[1] The Thessalonians are not to "grieve like the rest who have no hope," and this may be all one should understand behind their grief: a potential questioning of the resurrection.[2] With Augustine, "Nor ought you to sorrow as those heathens who have no hope, seeing that in regard to those friends, who are not lost, but only called earlier than ourselves to the country whither we shall follow them, we have hope, resting on a most sure promise, that from this life we shall pass into that other life, in which they shall be to us more beloved as they shall be better known, and in which our pleasure in loving them shall not be alloyed by any fear of separation."[3] Elsewhere, wrote Augustine: "[Paul] didn't just say *that you may not be saddened* but *that you may not be saddened like the heathen are, who do not have any hope*. It's unavoidable, after all, that you should be saddened; but when you feel sad, let hope console you."[4] Luther agreed, writing of a departed saint: "He is in a place which he would not wish to exchange for all the world, not even for a moment. Grieve in such a way, therefore, as to console yourselves even more. For you have not lost him, but have sent him on ahead of you to be kept in everlasting blessedness."[5] Luther elsewhere added: "It is little wonder if those are sad who have no hope. Nor can they be blamed for it. Since they are beyond the pale of faith in Christ, they must either

---

1. On the common secular skepticism of a bodily resurrection, see Ware, *Final Triumph*, 165–66.
2. Kim and Bruce, *Thessalonians*, 378–81.
3. Augustine, *Letter* 92.1 (*NPNF*[1] 1:380).
4. Augustine, *Sermon* 173.3 (*Works*, 5:255); emphasis in original.
5. Luther, "Letter 248," 52.

cherish this temporal life as the only thing worthwhile and hate to lose it, or they must expect that after this life they will receive eternal death and the wrath of God in hell and must fear to go there."[6]

"Hope" therefore frames the discussion (1 Thess 4:13; 5:8). Paul says that the dead in Christ "have fallen asleep" (and will wake up!), a biblical euphemism for death (Gen 47:30; Deut 31:16; 1 Kgs 2:10; Job 14:12-13; Ps 13:3; Jer 51:39-40; 2 Macc 12:45; John 11:11-13; Acts 13:36; 1 Cor 11:30; Homer, *Il.* 11.241; Sophocles, *El.* 509). Sleep is also an expression of resurrection hope (Dan 12:2; T. Jud. 25.4; T. Iss. 7.9; 2 Macc 12:44-45; 1 En. 91.10; 92.3). This concept would otherwise have seemed strange in the Greco-Roman world, as if it meant the animation of a corpse. Many pagans, however, affirmed some form of afterlife and not annihilation.[7]

The rest of humanity has no hope. For Paul, *grieving* as the rest is not problematic, but rather grieving in the *manner* of the rest. "Just as" suggests a comparison of degree rather than kind. Pagans have no positive hope for the afterlife and face judgment (1 Thess 1:10; 5:9). Paul contrasts believers and nonbelievers all through this section. Tertullian therefore commends a moderation in bereavement in view of that hope (*Pat.* 9). Basil the Great and Ambrose urge readers not to surrender to their sorrow and grief because of the resurrection hope.[8]

The conditional statement ("if we believe" in v. 14) *may* be an early Christian confession: thus it uses "Jesus" and *aneste*, not Paul's usual word for the resurrection (as in 1 Cor 15:3-5). "We believe" instead of "we know" suggests more than facts: the need for faith in affirming Jesus had risen again.

"Through Jesus" most naturally goes with "those who have fallen asleep" (since "with him" already modifies "will bring"). God acts "through Jesus" to bring with him (Jesus) those who have fallen asleep. Perhaps Jesus receives *the spirit* of the dying Christian, as Acts 7:59 suggests, but "through" (*dia*) Jesus may have the force of dying "in" (*en*) Jesus as a Christ believer (e.g., 1 Cor 15:18). Jesus is the agent of God's resurrection (likewise 1 Cor 15:21).

---

6. Luther, "Preface to the Burial Hymns," 325-26.

7. Ware, *Final Triumph*, 98-104.

8. Basil the Great, *Letter* 28 (*NPNF*[2] 8:132-33); Ambrose, *Exc.* 1.9; 2.3; also Ambrosiaster on 1 Thess 4:13-14 (*Commentaries*, 108). Jerome would also appeal to this passage to comfort believers, e.g., *Letter* 75.1 (*NPNF*[2] 6:155); *Vigil.* 6 (*NPNF*[2] 419); so also Aquinas, *Commentary*, 34-35 (on 4:13); Calvin, *Epistles*, 362-63; Poole, *Commentary*, 3:744.

Deceased Christians may be brought from heaven with Jesus or may be raised to be with Jesus at his return (with perhaps 2 Cor 4:14). Paul has been talking about Christ's return (1 Thess 1:10; 2:19; 3:13). The concern is whether the dead will be participating in these events. The point here is that God "brings" them from death to be *with* Jesus.[9] They were not with him already.

"The word of the Lord" in v. 15 is a Septuagintalism for someone speaking for God (e.g., 1 Kgs 13:1–5, 32; 21:17; 1 Chr 15:15; Ezek 34:1; 35:1; Hos 1:1; Sir 48:3, 5). This is not a direct quote of Jesus (like 1 Cor 7:10). Paul typically *paraphrases* Jesus's sayings, and the ideas here parallel Jesus's (in, e.g., Matt 16:25, 28; 24:31, 34; 26:64; Luke 13:30; John 5:25; 6:39–40; 11:25–26). Perhaps Paul views himself as a prophetic interpreter of the historical Jesus sayings and the OT with direct messages from the risen Lord, but he carefully distinguishes his *own* teaching from the words of the Lord in 1 Corinthians.[10] Paul is therefore most likely adapting Jesus's teaching.

One should not read too much into "we" since it is qualified as those living and left at that time. Paul did not know when he would die or whether he would be alive at Christ's "coming" (also 1 Cor 15:23 via Dan 7:13–14), nor is he claiming to know the timing of Christ's return. He is simply relaying what the situation will be for those who remain alive; so also, e.g., Theodore of Mopsuestia, Theodoret of Cyrus, Calvin.[11] Charles Wesley celebrated the imminent descent of Christ from heaven for all to see with a hymn, first published in 1758, that is still in many modern hymnals: "Lo! He Comes with Clouds Descending."

Verses 16c–17a repeat verbally and thematically v. 15b, perhaps with one or the other as a commentary on a fresh oracle or paraphrase of the Lord's teaching, whether that be in v. 15b or vv. 16c–17a. The fanfare with Christ's coming is reminiscent of Yahweh's descent in Exod 19:16, 18 (also Ps 47:5 [46:6 LXX]; Mic 1:3). Believers are "caught up" (also 2 Cor 12:2, 4). The meeting takes place in the clouds or air and not heaven ("air": Wis 5:11; 1 Cor 9:26). The trumpet blast dovetails with the day of the Lord (Isa 27:13; Joel 2:1; Zech 9:14; Sib. Or. 4.174; 1 Cor 15:52).

Verses 15–17 parallel 1 Cor 15:51–52: command given, the Lord descends, dead believers rise first, living believers rise, both groups meet

---

9. Kim and Bruce, *Thessalonians*, 384.

10. See the discussion of this point in Das, *Remarriage*, 61–63.

11. Theodore of Mopsuestia, *Commentaries*, 476–77; Theodoret of Cyrus, *Commentaries*, 2:118; Calvin, *Epistles*, 364–65.

Christ in the air, all will be with the Lord always. The scenario in vv. 16–17 (through 1 Thess 5:7) also parallels in many ways Matt 24:8, 30–49: Christ returns, from heaven, accompanied by angels, with a trumpet of God, believers are gathered to Christ, in clouds, at a time unknown, coming like a thief, unbelievers unaware of the coming judgment, judgment like a mother's birth pangs, believers are not to be deceived, and are to be watchful, warning against drunkenness.[12] Similarly, Dan 7:13–14 has "one like a son of man" either going up into the clouds to meet the Ancient of Days or coming with the clouds to meet God on earth for the judgment (like 1 Thess 4:14). Daniel 12:1's major distress "at that time" is followed by the deliverance of God's people as multitudes rise from their sleep to either everlasting life or shame. Paul, for his part, does not mention the resurrection of unbelievers, only of believers, and, with Augustine, it will be bodily.[13]

The dead in Christ rise *first*. "For dead Christians to join living Christians in a rapture to meet the Lord in the air, they will have to rise first."[14] Nothing is said about what happens next (but see 1 Cor 15). Again, Paul says nothing about nonbelievers, except for the future wrath of 1 Thess 5:9. The early third-century Tertullian stressed that God is perfectly able to raise the dead in the flesh (*Res.* 57). In a status-conscious society, the dead take priority over the living.

The key word in v. 17 is "meeting" (*apantēsin*), which is not a technical term.[15] Mikael Tellbe also questions an anti-imperial agenda in this passage.[16] Nevertheless, Cicero described Julius Caesar's victory tour in Italy in 40 BC: "What ovations [*apantēsis*] from the towns and what honour is paid him."[17] He wrote of Augustus: "The country towns are wonderfully enthusiastic for the boy. . . . There was a wonderful crowd to meet [*apantēsis*] him and cheer for him."[18] A greeting committee would escort the royal personage or dignitary into the city for the official visit.

---

12. Witherington, *Thessalonians*, 135–36.

13. Augustine, *Enarrat. Ps.* 3.5.

14. Kim and Bruce, *Thessalonians*, 381.

15. Cosby identifies missing elements in the reception motif ("Hellenistic Formal Receptions"). Robert Gundry has offered a rebuttal of each of Cosby's six points ("Brief Note"); see, in more detail, Gundry, "Hellenization," 161–69.

16. Tellbe, *Paul*, 123–40, esp. 127–30: still with "*strong connotations . . . of the coming of imperial visitors to a provincial city*" (129; emphasis in original).

17. Cicero, *Att.* 16.8.16.2 (Winstedt, LCL).

18. Cicero, *Att.* 16.11.16 (Winstedt, LCL).

Pompey and Octavian had visited Thessalonica, with the city as Pompey's capital in exile. As Chrysostom recognized: "For when a king drives into a city, those who are in honor go out to meet him; but the condemned await the judge within.... And as He descends, we shall go forth to meet Him, and, what is more blessed than all, so shall we be with Him."[19] Jesus is the object of similar rhetoric here, functioning *counter*-imperially, or better, transcending the earthly imperium. Caesar's empire is just a pale imitation in this redrawing of the universe's map.[20]

Whether Christ remains in the air or comes to earth, the point of the meeting is to be with the Lord and not escort duty (2 Cor 4:14).[21] Since believers do not go at their own initiative to meet the Lord but are snatched into the air, Gundry points out that believers cannot raise *themselves* into the air.[22] Apocalyptic literature often has the righteous "with" the Messiah in heaven (4 Ezra 14.9 [after the resurrection of the dead for judgment (7.29–32)]; 1 En. 39.6–7; 62.14; 71.16).[23] Paul does not narrate the believers' return with Christ to earth, although the Lord is moving *downward*.[24] Ultimately, interpreters point to a commonplace Hellenistic tradition of greeting the arriving dignitary in the Thessalonian world.

Kim and Bruce questioned the appeal to a Greco-Roman "meeting" of the arriving dignitary since the people are snatched up.[25] Gundry's response, however, was compelling, and Kim and Bruce ultimately conceded a potential reference to the Greco-Roman custom of meeting the arriving party: "Paul likely intends this," but modified by allusions also to the Sinaitic and Danielic theophanies.[26] Daniel 7 allusions appear to have motivated the departures from the usual Hellenistic meeting traditions to allow for God's snatching up.[27] On "caught up"/"snatched," see Acts 8:39; 23:10; 2 Cor 12:2–4; Rev 12:5. "In clouds" is theophanic in Exod 19:16–18; 24:15–18; 40:34; 1 Kgs 8:10–11; Ps 97:2. The point is that the believer will be *with the Lord* forever!

---

19. John Chrysostom, *Homilies on 1 Thessalonians* 8 (NPNF¹ 13:356).
20. Oakes, "Re-Mapping," 315, 317; Brookins, *Thessalonians*, 95–96.
21. Plevnik, "Destination"; Plevnik, *Paul*, 65–98.
22. Gundry, "Hellenization," 166; contra Malherbe, *Letters to the Thessalonians*, 277.
23. Brookins, *Thessalonians*, 102–3.
24. Oakes, "Re-Mapping," 316.
25. Kim and Bruce, *Thessalonians*, 395.
26. Kim and Bruce, *Thessalonians*, 404.
27. Kim and Bruce, *Thessalonians*, 406.

John Nelson Darby proposed a dispensational approach to these verses, and the "rapture" was popularized by the 1909 Scofield Reference Bible. Believers in Christ are rescued by their ascent to heaven.[28] In Darby's "premillennial" approach, Christ descends from the heavens to "snatch" believers away to heaven before a coming period of tribulation by the antichrist, all of which precedes Christ's return yet again for his earthly millennial rule. However, Paul does not ever describe a messianic kingdom on earth, even in 1 Cor 15:23–28, 51–57; Phil 3:20–21. Nothing suggests that to be "caught" into the air is to be snatched from a coming tribulation. In the apocalypses, the righteous either live through tribulation and are finally saved (1 En. 1.1–8; 10.17; 4 Ezra 5.1–13; 6.13–25; 7.27; 9.3–13; 13.48; 2 Bar. 25.1–4; 29.2; 1QM I, 11–12; XV, 1; Add Esth 11:2–12 LXX), or they are shielded during that time (2 Bar. 29.2; Sib. Or. 3.702–7). Although believers meet Christ in the air and Paul narrates no return to earth, Christ is nevertheless *descending* as he meets his followers.

The Thessalonians (v. 18) should encourage and comfort one another with these promises of a grand reunion of all believers in Christ and with him (on encouraging, see 1 Thess 5:11). The word sometimes means and is translated here as "comfort" rather than "exhort" (see P.Oxy. 115; 1 Thess 3:2, 7; 5:11; "exhort" in 1 Thess 2:12; 4:1, 10; 5:14).

---

28. Scofield, *Scofield Reference Bible*.

6

1 Thessalonians 5:1–11
Christ's Return for Those Living

Translation

[1] Now ABOUT THE times and seasons, brothers and sisters, you have no need to be written to, [2] because you yourselves know accurately that the day of the Lord so comes as a thief in the night. [3] When they say "peace and security," then sudden ruin will come upon them just like the labor pains of a pregnant woman, and they will by no means escape.

[4] But you, brothers and sisters, are not in darkness so that the day surprises you like a thief [5] since you all are sons of light and sons of day. We are not of night or of darkness. [6] So then, let us not sleep like the rest, but let us stay awake and be sober. [7] For those who sleep sleep at night, and those who get drunk get drunk at night. [8] But as for us, since we are of the day, let us be sober, by putting on the breastplate of faith and love and as a helmet the hope of salvation, [9] because God did not appoint us for wrath but for obtaining salvation through our Lord Jesus Christ, [10] who died for us so that, whether we are awake or asleep, we may live together with him. [11] Therefore, comfort one another and build each other up, one on one, just as you in fact are doing.

Commentary

In ch. 5 Paul continues to complete what is lacking in the Thessalonians' faith (1 Thess 3:10) as he turns from deceased Christians (4:13-18) to living ones (5:1-11). If some believers have died, is Christ's coming more distant? The Thessalonians had been eager to know when the day of the Lord would take place, and Paul assures them of their impending fate at the judgment as children of the day.

"Now about" with the vocative (of address) "brothers and sisters" signals a new topic (also 1 Thess 4:9, 13), in this case *related* to what Paul has been saying about the Lord's coming, but here an exhortation based on the Thessalonians' knowledge. Related topics (*de*) begin in vv. 4 and 8: unbelievers will be judged (vv. 1-3), believers are to be prepared (vv. 4-7), and God's elect people are to be faithful and encourage each other in view of the coming events (vv. 8-11).[1] The section concludes in v. 11.

This paragraph continues the emphatic contrast between the last chapter's "outsiders"/"the rest" vs. "you." Here the contrast is children of darkness vs. children of light. The Thessalonians have a different destiny than "the rest" (1 Thess 4:13). Christians are to act consistently with their identity given what is to come. Similar motifs—the imminent day of the Lord and his coming—are in Rom 13:11-14 with sleeping, waking, and sobriety language (preparing for that day [1 Cor 1:8]). This paragraph is *not* about events on earth after believers are caught up into the air as if they were taken away (1 Thess 4:13-18), since the instructions assume believers on earth. The phrase "with the Lord" in 4:17 and "with him" in 5:10 both assume the *same* single coming of the Lord that comforts believers in 4:18 and 5:11.[2]

"Times" (*chronos*) and "seasons" (*kairos*) are synonymous and are frequently used together as a hendiadys (two words for one thing to make it emphatic) for end-times events (Dan 2:21; 7:12; Sir 29:5; Neh 10:34 LXX [10:35 Eng.]; 13:31; Wis 8:8; Acts 1:7; 3:19-21). The Thessalonians do not need to know how long it will be before the events take place. Paul then explains in v. 2 *why* he does not need to write about the timing (*gar*): the Thessalonians already know ("you yourselves"), unlike the others of their world, but the reminder will be helpful.

---

1. Rigaux, "Tradition"; Richard, *Thessalonians*, 260-61; Beale, *Thessalonians*, 143; Witherington, *Thessalonians*, 144.

2. Witherington, *Thessalonians*, 144; Howard, "Literary Unity."

The "day of the Lord" is scriptural language usually employed for God's judgment (Job 20:28; Isa 2:12; 13:6-9, 13; 58:13; Jer 46:10; Ezek 7:10; Joel 1:15; 2:31; Amos 5:18-20 [darkness to some; light to others]; Obad 15-17 [against the nations but deliverance for Zion]; Zeph 1:14-18; 2:2-3; 3:8; Zech 12-14 [deliverance]; Rom 2:5 [day of wrath]), but now in reference to Christ. Like a thief in the night, the coming of the Lord will be a sudden, unpredictable intrusion into the world (Matt 24:42-44 // Luke 12:39; 2 Pet 3:10; Rev 3:3; 16:15; on thieves coming to destroy, see, e.g., Jer 49:9). The suddenness was emphasized already by early Christian authors (Cyprian, *Treatises* 12.3.89; Ambrose, *Of the Christian Faith* 5.17.210, 5.17.212) to encourage believers to stay alert (so also Theodore of Mopsuestia).[3] Did J. R. R. Tolkien's *Two Towers* draw from the fourth-century Ambrosiaster? "He will appear suddenly . . . , as the first ray of dawn from the east to the west, having with him the host of the army of God the Father" to destroy the armies of the antichrist.[4]

That they know "accurately" comes across as ironic overstatement since it is to be sudden and unexpected when others are celebrating "peace and security" in v. 3.[5] They have, however, already received "accurate" teaching to this effect. Chrysostom commented: "Do not be confident in thy youth, nor think that thou hast a very fixed term of life. . . . Dost thou not see men taken away prematurely day after day? . . . Affairs are full of much change. We are not masters of our end. Let us be masters of virtue."[6] Luther repeatedly counseled Michael Stiefel that Christ could come back before or after the various dates he was setting for the return.[7]

"When they say 'peace and security'" (v. 3) is reminiscent of what the false prophets of old say, "Peace, peace" (Jer 6:14; 8:11; Ezek 13:10, 16), but Paul does not cite these texts. The addition of the (non-Pauline) "security" points to a slogan "they" say. "Peace" (*pax*) and, separately, "security" (*securitas*) were on first-century Roman coins arguably in the time of Augustus.[8] A mid-first-century BC monument celebrated

---

3. Theodore of Mopsuestia, *Commentaries*, 480-83.

4. Gerald Bray, in Ambrosiaster, *Commentaries*, 109.

5. Brookins, *Thessalonians*, 106; Malherbe, *Letters to the Thessalonians*, 290; Fee, *Thessalonians*, 187.

6. John Chrysostom, *Homilies Concerning the Power of the Tempter* 2.5 (NPNF[1] 9:190); see also John Chrysostom, *Homilies on 1 Thessalonians* 9 (NPNF[1] 13:360).

7. Luther, *Letters of Spiritual Counsel*, 301-3.

8. Weima, "Peace and Security," 333-41.

Pompey's restoration of "peace and security" (SEG 46:1562).[9] After the civil war, in Praeneste (Palestrina, Italy), twin monuments were built celebrating peace and security. A Syrian inscription reads: "The Lord Marcus Flavius Bonus, the most illustrious Comes and Dux of the first legion, has ruled over us in peace and given constant peace and security to travelers and to the people" (*OGIS* 613).[10] Plutarch played on a popular recognition of this slogan to describe the "peace and security" promised by the enemy king Phraates to Marc Antony (*Ant.* 40.4). Tacitus (*Hist.* 3.53; 4.74) and Josephus (*A.J.* 14.9.1 §§158–160; 14.10.22 §§247–248; 15.10.1 §348) similarly described times of "security and peace."[11] Joel White nevertheless cautions that "security" is less prominent—and appearing for the first time as a phrase only in the latter years of Nero, and even here a Roman slogan may not be in view. The two words are not often paired, and "justice" and "well-being" are more typical.[12] *Greek* cities promised their inhabitants "security" as Paul correspondingly responds to both Roman peace and Greek security.[13] The stakes are simply higher with an impending *otherworldly* invasion.[14] Whether Roman or Greek propaganda, "sudden ruin will come upon them," echoing Jeremiah's "sudden" destruction. It will be for the complacent like "the *labor pains* of a pregnant woman," an image of judgment (Ps 48:6; Isa 26:16–19; 66:8; Jer 22:22–23; 30:6–7; 50:41–43; Mic 4:9–10; Luke 21:34–36). Paul is not "leading a social movement for reform" but anticipating God's ultimate intervention to right wrongs.[15] Thomas Aquinas stressed that it will be a time not of mercy but of justice.[16] Paul does, however, note the practical implications of his message for the behavior of the Christ-believing community toward outsiders.

Paul turns from the "they" of v. 3 to "you brothers and sisters" in vv. 4–5, who enjoy a very different fate. "You" are sons of light and the day. Note similar in-group descriptions at Qumran (1QS I, 9; II, 16; III, 13–27; 1QM I, 1–14). "Night's the time for thieves, daylight for

---

9. Weima, *Thessalonians*, 350.
10. Weima's translation ("Peace and Security," 352).
11. Witherington, *Thessalonians*, 146–47; Weima, *Thessalonians*, 348–51.
12. White, "Peace and Security" (2013).
13. White, "'Peace' and 'Security'" (2014).
14. Rightly Boring, *Thessalonians*, 180. On Epicurean principles as the background, see Malherbe, *Letters to the Thessalonians*, 304–6.
15. Witherington, *Thessalonians*, 147.
16. Aquinas, *Commentary*, 44.

honesty."[17] Darkness often symbolizes alienation from God (Job 22:9–11; Pss 27:1; 74:20; 82:5; 112:4; Prov 4:18–19; Isa 2:5; 9:2; 60:19–20; 1QS III, 13–26). Paul may be hinting at ignorance as well (Rom 1:21; 2:19; 1 Cor 4:5), in this case ignorance of that day's timing. Those in darkness will be surprised. That ignorance also expresses itself in immorality (vv. 6–8). William Tyndale in the sixteenth century drew on the language of this passage: Christ is coming "as a thief in the night," and so people are to be prepared, since those not of the faith will be destroyed and Christ's own delivered.[18]

"Sons" reflects a first-century patriarchal culture in which only males would inherit. In Christ the light has *already* dawned, and the Thessalonians have been transformed. The entire audience, even women (!), are sons of the light (similarly Isa 30:26; 60:19–20; Rom 13:12–13; 2 Cor 6:14–18). Images of light and darkness reinforce community membership and boundaries; the Thessalonians enjoy "inside" information about the events to come! They need not fear that "day."

With "so then" (v. 6) Paul turns to exhortation, still grounded in that contrast of destinies. The assurance of the Thessalonians' identity in vv. 4–5 grounds their actions in vv. 6–7. "The rest" are sleepers and drunkards, the latter of which may be a nod to the excesses of the Thessalonian Dionysiac cult.[19] (For the pairing "be awake" and "sober," see 1 Pet 5:8; "To an Uneducated Ruler," in Plutarch, *Mor.* 781D.) Sleep is a metaphor in v. 6 for the spiritually indifferent, but in v. 7 literal sleep and in v. 10 a euphemism for death (as in 1 Thess 4:14–15). Alertness is grounded in their new identity—thus the encouragement to *see oneself* in this way in v. 5. They are to keep awake and be ready for Christ's coming. To be sober is to be sober *minded* (also 1 Pet 1:13; 4:7; 5:8). With Clement of Alexandria: "We should sleep so as to be easily awakened.... For there is no use of a sleeping man, as there is not of a dead man. Wherefore we ought often to rise by night and bless God" (*Paed.* 2.9 [*ANF* 2:258]). The ancients did not enjoy modern artificial lighting and a "graveyard shift." Nighttime was for sleep and drunkenness with the children of darkness.

Note the contrast in v. 8 with "but as for us": Christ believers behave differently in preparation for his coming. With the sixth-century Latin hymn, still popular in modern hymnals, "Hark! a thrilling voice is

---

17. Euripides, *Iph. taur.* 1025–26 (trans. Vellacott; *"Alcestis" and Other Plays*, 162).
18. Tyndale, *Obedience*, 13.
19. Brocke, *Thessaloniki*, 128–29.

sounding: 'Christ is nigh!' it seems to say, 'Cast away the dreams of darkness, O ye children of the day!'"[20] The aorist participle "put on" follows the main verb and thus expresses simultaneous action.[21] Since the cause is expressed in the *prior* clause, the participial clause with its simultaneous action expresses the *means* by which "we" are to be sober, via the armor. Armor imagery is more detailed in Eph 6:14–17 (also Rom 6:13; 13:12; 2 Cor 6:7; 10:3–5; Phil 2:25; 2 Tim 2:3–4; Phlm 2). Calvin pointed to the continual battle before the end, requiring armor for the believer.[22] He added:

> It follows that dilatoriness is too fraught with danger. We note that, though otherwise given to indulgence, yet when the enemy is close, soldiers refrain from drunken sprees and all physical pleasures and keep careful watch. Since, therefore, Satan is ever pressing upon us, and threatening us with a thousand dangers, we ought at least to be no less diligent and watchful.[23]

Jeremy Taylor in the seventeenth century expanded on how the believer wages this war: through prayer, fasting, a cheap diet, and laborious exercises.[24]

Paul provides only *two* pieces of armor for the triad of faith, hope, and love (see 1 Thess 1:3; thus matching Isa 59:17; Wis 5:18–20). The most vulnerable part is the head, and hence the helmet of the hope of future salvation. The armor defends against vice (deeds of darkness)! Hope is stressed as the last in the series with its own piece of armor and with differing syntax from the others.[25] "*Because* God did not appoint us for (the future) wrath" (vv. 9–10; on wrath, see 1 Thess 1:10; 2:12; 3:3; on predestination, see Rom 8:29–30; 2 Thess 2:13), the Thessalonians are to put on this armor. Salvation, although enjoyed in the present, is often described as culminating in the *future*, a gift "obtained through our Lord Jesus Christ" to those who persevere in their deeds. Paul again addresses all the Thessalonians as "appointed," the language of gracious election and a new identity.

---

20. Caswall, "Hark!," st. 1.
21. Porter, *Verbal Aspect*, 381.
22. Calvin, *Epistles*, 369–70.
23. Calvin, *Epistles*, 369.
24. Taylor, "Holy Living," 67–69.
25. Malherbe, *Letters to the Thessalonians*, 298.

Christ died "for" or "on behalf of us" in order that believers may live together with him. The parallels between 1 Thess 4:14–18 and 5:1–11 indicate that the paragraphs are not sequential but rather encouragement for Christ's one return. To be "with the Lord" is Pauline participatory language that is otherwise absent in the Thessalonian correspondence: Christ's death *for* believers allows them to be (together) *with* him.[26] "Clearly we have here all the essential elements of Paul's doctrine of justification by God's grace in Christ's vicarious death, including faith."[27] Awake and asleep in v. 10 refer to those who "live with him" rather than the insider-outsider distinction dominating vv. 6–7. "Whether we are awake or asleep" also signals that Paul did not know if he would be living at the time of Christ's return.

With "therefore" (v. 11) referring back to vv. 1–10, Paul offers two imperatives. They are to comfort one another (also 1 Thess 4:18) and "build each other up," echoing what God did for Israel (Jer 24:6; 31:4 [38:4 LXX]; 33:7 [40:7 LXX]; 42:10 [49:10 LXX]) and what apostles and Christians are now to do (1 Cor 8:1; 14:3–4, 17; 2 Cor 10:8; 12:19; 13:10). "One on one" is an odd phrase and suggests greater intimacy than a mere assembly.[28] In 1 Thess 2:11 as well, Paul treated them as individuals ("each one" [*hena hekaston*]).

---

26. Brookins, *Thessalonians*, 112.

27. Kim and Bruce, *Thessalonians*, 437, noting the *dik-* terminology (1 Thess 4:6), blamelessness (3:13; 5:23), and wrath (1:10; 2:16).

28. Malherbe, *Letters to the Thessalonians*, 131. See "one on one" in Theocritus, *Id.* 22.65.

7

1 Thessalonians 5:12–28
General Exhortations and Closing

Translation

[12] Now we request of you brothers and sisters to recognize those laboring among you and caring for you in the Lord and admonishing you, [13] and to esteem them highly in love on account of their work. Be at peace among yourselves. [14] And we are exhorting you brothers and sisters to admonish the disorderly, encourage the discouraged, be devoted to the weak, be patient with everyone. [15] See that no one repays evil, but always pursue what is good for one another and for everyone.

[16] Rejoice always; [17] pray constantly; [18] give thanks in everything, since this is the will of God for you in Christ Jesus. [19] Do not quench the Spirit, [20] do not despise prophecies, [21] but test everything; cling to the good, [22] abstain from every evil kind of evil.

[23] Now may the God of peace himself make you completely holy, and may your whole spirit and soul and body be kept blameless at the coming of our Lord Jesus Christ. [24] Faithful is the one calling you, who will indeed do it.

[25] Brothers and sisters, pray also for us. [26] Greet all the brothers and sisters with a holy kiss. [27] I adjure you by the Lord to have the letter read to all the brothers and sisters. [28] The grace of our Lord Jesus Christ be with you.

Commentary

Paul begins in v. 12 a series of general exhortations that will continue through v. 22, consisting largely of short imperatives—fifteen of them, with two infinitives with imperatival force, all creating a staccato effect (perhaps easier to memorize).[1] The section generally parallels Rom 12:9-18; also Phil 4:2-9. The parallels to other Pauline passages suggest a distinctive, common paraenesis (exhortation). The echoes of Jesus's teaching further suggest a body of traditional Christian paraenesis now being shaped by Paul for the Thessalonians (although note the lack of parallel for vv. 12-13a in Rom 12).[2] Community life, leadership, and witness "in the Lord" are the topics of this section.

Verses 12-15 are parallel: introductory formula (we ask you, we urge you, see to it), command/request (to acknowledge and to regard, admonish . . . encourage . . . help, that no one repays), summary command (be at peace, be patient, always pursue the good), and target of behavior (among yourselves, toward all such people, toward one another and toward all). A single article governs vv. 12-13, identifying a single object for those given recognition, whether all believers or the leaders at Thessalonica who are "laboring"; hard physical labor (1 Cor 4:12; 2 Cor 6:5; 11:23, 27; 1 Thess 2:9; 2 Thess 3:8); laboring for the gospel/church (1 Cor 15:10, 58; 2 Cor 10:15; Gal 4:11; Phil 2:16; Col 1:29; 1 Thess 1:3; 3:5).[3]

A *prostatis* (one caring) refers to a patron in Rom 16:1-2 (Phoebe) and not one who "presides over" others.[4] In Rom 12:8 the same verb is in a context of sharing material resources and mercy, thus leaders in the sense of patrons, caregivers, and protectors.[5] Their nonformal guidance derives from benevolent patriarchy; e.g., 1 Tim 3:4, 5, 12; 5:17; Titus 3:8, 14.[6] Note also the parallels with 1 Cor 16:15-18 and Stephanas's household that served others in leadership. Respect and "esteem" those who are laboring for their work within the community and with the love that

---

1. Kim and Bruce, *Thessalonians*, 455.
2. Brookins, *Thessalonians*, 116; Wanamaker, *Thessalonians*, 191.
3. Malherbe, *Letters to the Thessalonians*, 310-11; Brookins, *Thessalonians*, 117.
4. See the stress on priestly leadership in, e.g., John Chrysostom, *Homilies on 1 Thessalonians* 10 (NPNF[1] 13:366).
5. Witherington, *Thessalonians*, 160.
6. Meeks, *First Urban Christians*, 134. Weima stresses on the basis of parallel language in the Pastorals that they were "ruling over" the congregation (*Thessalonians*, 384-85).

characterizes the believers' relationships (similarly Rom 12:5–8; 1 Cor 16:15–16). They are to "be at peace" (also Rom 12:18; 2 Cor 13:11). In these Christ-believing assemblies, status apparently depends on the functions that were rendered.[7]

"We urge you" in v. 14 signals a new topic. "Urge" is the harshest form of Pauline exhortation.[8] *Ataktos* is to be disordered or unruly and not in line with the teaching but is used of the "idle" in 2 Thess 3:6–11 (three times) and is interchangeable with *argein* (to be idle) in Hellenistic papyri.[9] Unruly or "out-of-line" (insubordinate) behavior seems to be at issue in this context, especially with regard to those providing leadership in vv. 12–13, but the admonitions in 1 Thess 4:11–12 may point to idleness.

"Discouraged" means "fainthearted," a diffident person with a sense of inadequacy and not self-confident—thus a need to be encouraged.[10] Paul himself is encouraging the Thessalonians in, e.g., 1 Thess 1:6; 2:14; 3:3–4.

The "weak" may be so physically due to persecution since Paul has already spoken of emotional and spiritual weakness (1 Thess 3:1–10). They could be financially in need or concerned about the timing of Christ's return.[11] They are to be patient with each other and with everyone (also Gal 5:22; Eph 4:2; Col 1:11; 3:12–13). Christians are to watch out for each other in their communities, behaviorally and otherwise. Faith in Christ is no private matter.

They are not to repay evil to *anyone* (v. 15). The switch to a third-person admonition may signal that this is a recognizable aphorism. Vengeance belongs to God in biblical tradition (Deut 32:35; Prov 20:22; Rom 12:17, 19). Even "outsiders" ("for everyone") are neighbors, thus broadening the admonition; see the similar instructions about the treatment of enemies in Rom 5:6–11; 12:14, 17, 20; 1 Cor 15:8–10; 2 Cor 5:18–21. The Thessalonians are not just to refrain from retaliation but also do good to everyone. In the face of the severe ostracism and abuse faced at Thessalonica, such love, expressed by doing good to one's enemies, is exceedingly difficult.

---

7. Kim and Bruce, *Thessalonians*, 460–61.
8. Malherbe, *Letters to the Thessalonians*, 316—and at the head of a list of directions.
9. Milligan, *Thessalonians*, 152–54; e.g., P.Oxy. 4.725.
10. Witherington, *Thessalonians*, 162.
11. Witherington, *Thessalonians*, 163; Wanamaker, *Thessalonians*, 197–98; Weima, *Thessalonians*, 394–95.

1 THESSALONIANS 5:12–28

Verses 16–22 begin with prayer ("rejoice always") and end with prophecies. God's will is expressed in *all* the admonitions of vv. 16–18 since they are grouped together, with each beginning with a temporal reference ("always," "constantly") and with similar structure. Rejoicing, praying, and thanking (key elements of personal piety) are frequently grouped elsewhere in Paul (Phil 1:3–4; 4:4–6; 1 Thess 3:9–10).[12]

They are to rejoice *always*, and not just in worship. They rejoice even in troubles and persecution because of what they enjoy in the Lord (Rom 12:12; 14:17; Gal 5:22; Phil 2:18; 3:1; 4:4, 10; 1 Thess 1:6; 2:14–15, 19–20; 3:9).

Pray without ceasing (v. 17) calls them to a regular, diligent practice (Rom 12:12; Phil 1:4; 4:6). It is a prescription against worry and is Paul's own practice (1 Thess 1:2; 2:13). Prayer is not just to be lip service but wholehearted. John Cassian warned against praying in a distracted fashion as not really praying.[13] John Calvin likewise commented that unceasing prayer brings lasting joy through relief from afflictions and thus should be without ceasing.[14] Such prayer leads to a calm mind and a spirit of rejoicing.

Give thanks "in everything" (v. 18), no matter the circumstances (*en panti*)—not a temporal "always" as in v. 16; in every way/everything (1 Cor 1:5; 2 Cor 4:8; 6:4; 11:6, 9; Phil 4:6, 12). This is petitionary prayer, since thanksgiving is mentioned separately.[15] Paul says nothing about *what* one is praying or thanking for. Rather, give thanks *in* and not *for* all things, e.g., thankful *in* one's trials. "This is God's will in Christ Jesus."

On "rejoice, pray, and give thanks" in vv. 16–18, Athanasius commented:

> For no one is going to turn away from sin and start behaving righteously unless he thinks about what he is doing. Not until he has been straightened out by practicing godly behavior will he actually possess the reward of faith: the crown of righteousness that Paul possessed, having fought the good fight. That crown is laid up not just for Paul but for all who are like him in this respect. This sort of meditation and exercise in godliness should be familiar to us, as it was to the saints of old. It should be especially so in the season when the divine Word calls upon

---

12. Fee, *Thessalonians*, 215.
13. Cassian, *Second Conference of Abbot Isaac* 12–13 (*NPNF*[2] 11:1014–35).
14. Calvin, *Epistles*, 374–75.
15. Kim and Bruce, *Thessalonians*, 474.

us to keep the feast. For what, after all, is the feast but continual worship of God, recognition of godliness and unceasing prayer all done from the heart in full agreement with each other?[16]

Fire is a regular metaphor for the Spirit (Rom 12:11–12; 2 Tim 1:6), and thus Paul's "quench" in v. 19. Compare this with the burning fire shut up in Jeremiah's bones (Jer 20:9) when he could not prophesy. The Thessalonians do not seem as interested in prophecy, the opposite approach of the Corinthians. "Despising" is a strong way of phrasing their attitude/disdain for the spiritual gift (Gal 4:14). The Thessalonians are to test the prophecy, holding fast to what is good and staying away from the evil—whether understood as every *kind* or what *appears* to be—as they "cling to the good" (similarly Isa 1:16–17). The emphasis could be on v. 21, in which case they need to sift/test prophecies *more critically*. In staying away from evil, this is more than just testing of the prophetic utterances but is also to be moral discernment. Praying and prophecy are together in 1 Cor 11, a natural connection as communication. For Augustine, such prophesy is to expound Scripture; so also Ambrosiaster and Calvin.[17]

Verses 23–28, the letter closing, consist of a wish prayer/peace benediction (vv. 23–24), prayer request (v. 25), greeting (v. 26), request to read the letter (v. 27), and benediction (v. 28). These elements are also in Hellenistic letters—except that Paul focuses on spiritual rather than physical well-being.[18] Pauline letter closings summarize key concerns of the letter.

"May the God of *peace* make you completely *holy*" (also Rom 15:13, 33; 16:20; 1 Cor 14:33; 2 Cor 13:11; Phil 4:9)—as opposed to the unsanctified problems caused by the idle (1 Thess 4:11–12; 5:13; 2 Thess 3:16). Real holiness does not cause divisions but brings peace, reiterating 1 Thess 3:11–13. On the God of peace, see also the letter opening (1:1). Note the emphatic parallelism of "whole" and "completely." The call to sanctified living has dominated the exhortative section of the letter (4:1–5:22) but figured also earlier (e.g., 2:10, 12; 3:13).

"Spirit and soul and body" is the only apparent New Testament tripartite division of human nature. Origen justified multiple layers of

---

16. "Festal Letter 9," in Athanasius, *Resurrection Letters*, 157.

17. Augustine, *Enarrat. Ps.* (on Ps. 77[76]:4); Ambrosiaster, *Commentaries*, 111; Calvin, *Epistles*, 377.

18. Brookins, *Thessalonians*, 128.

meaning in biblical interpretation on the basis of a spirit-soul-body distinction (*Princ.* 4.1.11–13). Hebrews 4:12 distinguishes *psyche* and *pneuma* (see 1 Cor 15:45; Phil 1:27). Paul is not likely distinguishing higher inner faculties (spirit) from lower inner faculties such as impulses and affections (soul). Paul uses *psychikos* and *psyche* for the life force or being. The *psychikos* person is not "soulish" but the natural person apart from the Spirit. Adam became a "living being" (*psychē zosan* [Gen 2:7 LXX]), thus "life breath." The *pneuma* is the *non*material portion. Nevertheless, Thomas Aquinas rightly emphasized that this verse regards the whole human person.[19] "Put your heart and soul into it."[20]

The faithful God is the one busy, graciously at work accomplishing all this (Deut 7:9; Isa 49:7; Rom 8:30; Phil 1:6)! God will indeed prepare them as a holy people for Christ's coming (eight times in the letter! [1 Thess 1:10; 2:19; 3:13; 4:13–18; 5:1–11]).

Paul *asks for* prayer in v. 25, even as in 1 Thess 1:2 he always prays for them and just prayed for them in vv. 23–24 (2 Thess 3:1; Rom 15:30–32; 2 Cor 1:11; Eph 6:12–20; Phil 1:19; Col 4:3, 18; Phlm 22). He does not say why, whether it is to carry on his gentile mission (1 Thess 2:16), to remain steadfast in the face of persecution (3:17), and/or to return to Thessalonica (3:10–11).

On Paul's regular greeting with a holy kiss (v. 26), see Rom 16:16; 1 Cor 16:20; 2 Cor 13:12; also 1 Pet 5:14—perhaps on the cheek and not on the mouth (see also Mark 14:45; Luke 7:45; 15:20; 22:47–48; Acts 20:37). This was family hospitality expressed within gatherings of brothers and sisters in Christ. Paul may be asking the letter carrier to greet them all with a kiss on his behalf.[21] The kiss was maintained in the second and third centuries of Christianity (e.g., Justin Martyr, *1 Apol.* 65; Hippolytus, *Trad. ap.* 4.1; 18.3; 22.6; *Const. ap.* 2.7.57). They are to greet *all* the brothers and sisters (and not "one another")—thus not just a smaller group (church leadership?), but also those absent when the letter was read and between the house churches (see v. 27).[22] The admonition ("all the brothers and sisters") is repeated in v. 27, where it does not mean

---

19. Aquinas, *Commentary*, 53; Kim and Bruce, *Thessalonians*, 491–92—but the body would be *included*.

20. Thiselton, *Thessalonians*, 162. Contra Erasmus, "Enchiridion," 318–19; Luther, "Epistle to the Hebrews," 96, 158.

21. Furnish, *Thessalonians*, 125.

22. Brookins, *Thessalonians*, 131.

"each other," and Paul has in mind Christians *beyond* the primary recipients, i.e., primarily those in the Thessalonica environs.[23]

Verse 27's "I, Paul" suggests that Paul is taking up the pen here or even as early as v. 25 (thus the sudden shift to the first person) (1 Cor 16:21; Gal 6:11; 1 Thess 2:18; 3:5; 2 Thess 3:17; Phlm 19). The letter is to be read aloud and heeded. It is not just to be read by the leadership or left in only one house church. Paul wants the letter circulated.[24] That "brothers and sisters" is without qualification militates against church gatherings *too* far away. The absence of some at the first reading of the letter was a possibility when people often worked seven days a week, morning, noon, and night. Paul "adjures" the letter be read to all (Mark 5:7; Acts 19:13; Col 4:17; Josephus, *A.J.* 8.15.4 §404). Likely, new house churches were springing up beyond the original congregation(s) (as in Rom 16:5, 14–15).[25] Perhaps there had been some division or resistance from the disorderly (1 Thess 5:14), and Paul wants *them* to hear the letter.[26]

The shift to "I" again indicates that Paul is the primary author of this letter (note the shifts at 1 Thess 2:18; 3:5). Paul began by wishing them God's grace and closes that way in v. 28. On closing with an emphasis on grace (the grace benediction) as a Pauline convention, see Rom 16:20; 1 Cor 16:23; Gal 6:18; Phil 4:23; 2 Thess 3:18; Phlm 25.

---

23. Malherbe, *Letters to the Thessalonians*, 341–42.
24. Brookins, *Thessalonians*, 132–33.
25. Malherbe, *Letters to the Thessalonians*, 344–45.
26. Weima, *Thessalonians*, 427–30; Kim and Bruce, *Thessalonians*, 498.

8

2 Thessalonians 1:1–12
Thanksgiving and the Coming Judgment

Translation

[1] PAUL AND SILVANUS and Timothy to the church of the Thessalonians in God our Father and the Lord Jesus Christ. [2] Grace to you and peace from God [our] Father and the Lord Jesus Christ.

[3] We are obligated always to give thanks to God for you, brothers and sisters, just as is fitting, because your faith is flourishing and the love of each one of you all for one another is increasing, [4] so that we ourselves boast in you among the churches of God about your endurance and faith in all your persecutions and the sufferings which you are enduring; [5] [this is] evidence of the just judgment of God so that you would be counted worthy of the kingdom of God, for which you are also suffering, [6] since it is just in God's sight to repay your afflicters with affliction [7] and to you who are being afflicted [with] relief with us at the revelation of the Lord Jesus from heaven with the angels of his power [8] in a fire of flame, inflicting punishment on those who do not know God and on those not obeying the gospel of our Lord Jesus; [9] such people will pay a penalty of eternal ruin away from the presence of the Lord and from the glory of his might, [10] whenever he comes to be glorified among his holy ones and to be marveled at by all who have believed (because our testimony to you was believed), on that day.

[11] For this, we also are always praying for you all that our God may make you worthy of the calling and may complete every desire of goodness and work of faith in power, [12] so that the name of the Lord Jesus may be glorified in you, and you in him, according to the grace of our God and the Lord Jesus.

Commentary

"Paul and Silas and Timothy" (v. 1)—identical to 1 Thess 1:1—may indicate authorship not long after the writing of 1 Thessalonians. Paul again is the primary voice and thus the switch at times to "I" (2 Thess 2:5; 3:17; 1 Thess 2:18; 3:5; 5:27), but all three are in agreement. Sometimes, the "we" is genuinely plural (2 Thess 1:3–4, 11; 2:1, 13; 3:1, 4, 6, 7, 11, 14). The same issues (persecution, the day of the Lord, the unruly idlers) and the same three co-senders support that this letter was written not long after the first.[1]

"Church" means "assembly," and here it is the Thessalonian assembly gathering in the name of God the Father and the Lord Jesus Christ. As with 1 Thessalonians, this is a gathering of the *people* rather than in a place, which reinforces their identity: they are *God's* people at Thessalonica. Another potential rationale for such an address may be the coins minted at Thessalonica under Augustus with Julius Caesar on one side and a laurel wreath with the inscription "God" (*THEOS*) and "Thessalonians" (*THESSALONIKEŌN*) on the other. A later coin replaced Julius Caesar on the one side with Augustus, under the same legend, and a still-later coin had Tiberius. Paul would be co-opting imperial rhetoric for Christ.

Paul brings greetings from both God the Father and the Lord Jesus Christ, the double object of a single preposition. Both are ascribed the same qualities—both sources of grace and peace in what is a high Christology.[2] The Thessalonian "brothers and sisters" (already in v. 3) enjoy a new family through their relationship with God as their Father! Paul opens the letter with "peace" and will likewise close it (2 Thess 3:16, with emphasis). Giving thanks or sacrifice to a god was a cultural commonplace and is fitting here for the Thessalonians (v. 3; so also 2:13). Perhaps "we are *obligated* to give thanks" (note the lack of "are obligated"

---

1. Kim and Bruce, *Thessalonians*, 502.
2. Malherbe, *Letters to the Thessalonians*, 380; Weima, *Thessalonians*, 439.

in 1 Thess 1:2–3) and "as is fitting" are liturgical expressions.³ If so, the words would be emphatic.⁴

The thanksgiving section continues through v. 12 as Paul commends the Thessalonians in the midst of persecution (vv. 3–4), comforts them with the coming judgment and vindication (vv. 5–10), and challenges them to live up to a standard of conduct fitting for Christ believers as Paul prays for God's enablement (vv. 11–12). For the Pauline thanksgiving convention, see Rom 1:8–10; 1 Cor 1:4–9; 2 Cor 1:3–8; Phil 1:3–6.⁵

Paul is thankful for the mutual love and faith the Thessalonians are demonstrating toward each other. Their "flourishing" faith is, literally, growing greatly.⁶ Paul attributes these traits to the entire congregation(s). Whereas 1 Thess 3:10 flagged something as lacking in their faith, nothing appears to be lacking here. The "idlers" in 3:6–15 are apparently a minority, or Paul wants love to dominate the correction of these brothers and sisters.⁷

The result of their faith and love has been Paul's boasting in them (v. 4), especially as they persevere in their trials. He emphasizes "we ourselves" perhaps because they had been reluctant to boast of themselves or did not feel themselves worthy.⁸ Paul does not identify of which churches he had boasted. Boasting *in the Lord*, or in what the Lord has done, is commendable, but not a boasting in self or the flesh (1 Cor 4:7; 2 Cor 10:8–13; 12:5–9—Paul will ironically indulge in self-praise with respect to weaknesses, disasters, and trials).

When Paul refers to multiple assemblies or churches, as he does in this verse, he likely refers to all the churches he had started, whether at Thessalonica or elsewhere. The singular "church" could also be collective.

"Persecutions" and "tribulations," used together, amplify the sense of what the Thessalonians are enduring, whether physical, mental, or emotional. The final clause indicates that this situation is ongoing. Paul's comforting with the sure hope of salvation in the verses that follow points

---

3. Aus, "Liturgical Background."
4. Kim and Bruce, *Thessalonians*, 506.
5. Weima, *Thessalonians*, 441.
6. "It is not the kind of trait or the precise word that someone imitating Paul would easily pick up" (Best, *Thessalonians*, 250).
7. Weima, *Thessalonians*, 453.
8. Malherbe, *Letters to the Thessalonians*, 386.

to *greater* persecution than earlier.[9] "Faith," not "faithfulness," is the usual pairing with "endurance"—the trust necessary to endure persecution.

The meaning of "evidence" or "sign" (v. 5) is disputed. The word is not used elsewhere in the NT and here can be nominative (elliptical, assuming "which is") or accusative. An ellipsis could be filled in with a retrospective "this is . . . ," an accusative in direct apposition to what preceded; note the construction in Phil 1:28 (which suggests that the whole prior clause is in view here too). If so, it is not clear how the Thessalonians' endurance/perseverance connects to the righteous judgment of God without assuming that God has granted the Thessalonians this ability to persevere.[10] A prospective reading is also possible: "*Here is* the evidence of the just judgment of God . . ." followed by that evidence (see Rom 2:5). In other words, those who suffer should be reassured that *God will vindicate them*—thus vv. 6–10. This is a sign to help the persecuted endure. They will be counted worthy (divine passive) (similarly 1 Thess 2:16).[11]

The divine passive points to God as the active agent who will render the Thessalonians worthy (also 1 Cor 6:9–10; Gal 5:21). God is the active agent throughout this paragraph.[12] The day of the Lord has not yet come as the Thessalonians endure suffering. Some might have thought that severe suffering was proof that that day had passed them by, since the day of the Lord is associated with wrath in 1 Thess 5:2–3.[13]

Kim and Bruce sketch the logic: the persecutors sin against God by their actions, and believers prove their genuine faith by their endurance; there will be God's just judgment; those who believe will be justified, and sinners without the obedience of faith will be condemned. Believers will be saved at the last judgment and persecutors punished.[14]

In vv. 6–7 Paul contrasts the lost with the saved, and then in vv. 8–9 the fate of the lost with, in v. 10, the fate of those saved in an eschatological reversal of situations. Similar expectations are in Isa 66:6 LXX with the voice of God rendering recompense to enemies (also Prov 24:12 LXX). No doubt ("since") it is just of God to repay those troubling you with trouble (Deut 32:35).

---

9. Kim and Bruce, *Thessalonians*, 510.
10. Wanamaker, *Thessalonians*, 221.
11. Kim and Bruce, *Thessalonians*, 522.
12. Marshall, *Thessalonians*, 173, 182.
13. Bassler, "Enigmatic Sign," 508–9.
14. Kim and Bruce, *Thessalonians*, 517.

The Thessalonians are afflicted, as are Paul and his companions (v. 7). The repayment here echoes Isa 66:15's "flames of fire" in the context of the repayment of Isa 66:4. The "Lord" who repays is Yahweh in Isa 66 but Jesus here, another instance of Paul's divine Christology on display.[15] Christ's power to execute the just judgment of God is mediated here by the angels of his power.

Jesus's returning "in a fire of flame" (v. 8) is reminiscent of the burning bush theophany in Exod 3:2 and Acts 7:30 (also Ps 104:4; Isa 29:6; 30:30; 66:15; Dan 7:9). There will be "punishment," an echo of Isa 66:15–16 again where Yahweh comes like fire, but also 2 Sam 22:48; Ps 18:47 [17:48 LXX]; Rom 12:19—connections attesting to Paul's high Christology. Despite the repeated definite article before "those not obeying," both articles are with respective nouns describing the same group: non–Christ believers. Sometimes Jews—usually considered those who know God—are described in the Scriptures as *not* knowing God (e.g., Isa 1:3; Jer 4:22; 9:3–6; Hos 5:4). Disobedience and rejection may characterize gentiles (Ps 79:6; Jer 10:25; 1 Thess 4:5), but they characterize *both* Jews and gentiles in Rom 10:16 and 11:30–32. This is Hebraic synonymous parallelism (e.g., Jer 10:25) for those who refuse to acknowledge God (Isa 66:4; Rom 1:18–32; 10:16)—and not just the Thessalonians' persecutors, as the parallelism with v. 9 shows.

Their penalty (*dikēn* [v. 9]) is "eternal ruin," the same phrase as in 4 Macc 10:15 (the same sentiment without "eternal" appears in 1 Cor 5:5; 1 Thess 5:3; 1 Tim 6:9). For eternal *punishment* (and thus not annihilation), see Matt 25:46; 4 Macc 10:11, 15; 1QS II, 15; V, 13.[16] For destruction, see Pss. Sol. 2.31, 34–35; 15.12. The verse also echoes Isa 2:10, 19, 21 with the unrighteous trying to hide themselves in rocks from the Lord's presence (two parallels: "from the face of the Lord" and "from the glory of his might"). What is at stake, then, is eternal exclusion from God's presence. The punishment "would be meaningless if the punished were not conscious of their separation from the Lord's presence."[17] "To experience forever the absence of the God who is holy love is hell indeed."[18] Paul does not see any second chance beyond this life. For the saved, the result is glorification and transformation.

---

15. Hurtado, *Lord Jesus Christ*, 112, 112n79.
16. Malherbe, *Letters to the Thessalonians*, 402.
17. Kim and Bruce, *Thessalonians*, 532.
18. Witherington, *Thessalonians*, 197.

Apo may be causal: "by his presence and glory" (thus Jer 4:26), but the preposition is more typically spatial (esp. with, as here, "from the presence of" [*prosopou*], e.g., Acts 5:41; 7:45; Rev 12:14; 20:11), again consistent with the allusion to Isa 2:10, 19, 21 as the unrighteous hide from the Lord's face. Those who *do* know the Lord and who obey the gospel will enjoy the Lord's presence forever, enjoying the glory from which the others have been separated.[19] Paul warns of being shut out from the Lord's presence for eternity. That "fear" is not mentioned (as in Isa 2:10, 19, 21) should not be stressed, since the omission is likely a function of better parallelism with "from the glory of his might." Paul's high Christology is again on display, as the Isaiah passage regarding Yahweh is understood in terms of the "Lord Jesus" (1 Thess 3:13; 4:6; 2 Thess 1–7:8, 12).[20]

This is the darkest passage in the Pauline Letters about the dire fate of the punished. Vengeance and vindication, however, belong not to a human individual but to the Lord. The Lord will one day right the wrongs (Lev 19:18; Rom 12:19–20). The Thessalonians, then, should continue in faith and persevere.

God is not just merciful but also just and an avenger, not indifferent to the suffering of the afflicted. Theodore of Mopsuestia in the fourth century wrote: "Indeed, if a punishment remains for those who have failed only to obey the faith, how much more for those who call down false accusations and assaults on those who believe. . . . For he shows how heavy the torments are by what they are like, since the destructions are exterminations that accomplish ruin in time, yet are not temporal but for eternity."[21] Chrysostom recognized how offensive hell was even in his own time (fourth century), and yet a constant remembrance of the danger of hell is important in order to avoid it. He added that those standing before Christ's judgment seat will not be grateful that others avoided the topic or were silent about what would be coming. Hell is not temporary, said Chrysostom.[22] For Augustine, even the last day of one's own life is to be feared since it immediately precedes appearance before the judgment.[23] The contrast of everlasting bliss with everlasting punishment

---

19. Favoring annihilationism, see Fudge, "Final End," 333; contending for "cause" and not separation, see Quarles, "'APO.'"
20. Hurtado, *Lord Jesus Christ*, 112, 112n79.
21. Theodore of Mopsuestia, *Commentaries*, 500–501 (Commentary 2.45–46).
22. John Chrysostom, *Homilies on 2 Thessalonians* 2 (on 1:8) (NPNF¹ 13:382–84).
23. Letter 199.2, in Augustine, *Letters*.

would continue through the centuries with regular reference to 2 Thess 1's eternal separation.[24] The seventeenth-century Thomas Vincent wrote one of the darkest passages on the eternal punishment of these verses (*Fire and Brimstone*)—or, for that matter, John Milton's *Paradise Lost* has a horrible dungeon and a flaming furnace.[25] Matthew Poole, likewise in the seventeenth century, stressed that this is eternal *punishment* and not annihilation; so also John Wesley.[26]

God loves people even when they are enemies (Rom 5:8–10). In the face of a refusal of that love, there is no longer mercy but justice for the sake of the persecuted. This judgment on the persecutors will bring relief to Paul and the Thessalonians (2 Cor 2:13; 7:5; 8:13)—but it will not come until Christ's return, and thus must be "revealed" (1 Cor 1:7; 1 Thess 4:16).

More positively in v. 10, unlike those removed from his presence, Jesus comes to be glorified in the presence of the "holy ones." By "holy ones," Paul means saints rather than angels as is clear from the parallelism of vv. 10–12 with 2 Thess 2:13–14, which confirms that Christ believers are in view. He will be *with* them. They will marvel.[27] Witherington opines that "saints" refers to *Jewish* Christ believers whereas "believers" refers to gentiles.[28] Others identify the saints with (deceased) believers. See the reference to the "holy ones" returning with Christ in 1 Thess 3:13, where the phrase may refer to angels—some of the same issues in identification as here.

"Glorified in his holy ones/saints" alludes to Ps 89:5 (88:6 LXX). The saints reflect Jesus's glory in their lives or glorify him if "in" bears an instrumental sense, which is likely since the parallel clause is what believers *do* in marveling at the Lord.[29] "In" would make little sense had Paul had angels in mind in his echo of Ps 89:7 (88:8 LXX), where the word means "in."[30] Fee stresses that "in" the saints signals an "in your face" to the Thessalonians' persecutors. The persecutors will be there at the day

24. E.g., Calvin, *Institutes* 3.18.7; 3.25.4; 3.25.12.

25. Vincent, *Fire and Brimstone*, 31–35, 39–46 (chs. 5, 8); Milton, *Paradise Lost*, bk. 1, paras. 53–67.

26. Poole, *Commentary*, 3:756; J. Wesley, *Explanatory Notes*, 2.697; also the eighteenth-century Edwards, "Sinners."

27. Kim and Bruce, *Thessalonians*, 534.

28. Witherington, *Thessalonians*, 197.

29. Witherington, *Thessalonians*, 197.

30. Fee, *Thessalonians*, 261.

of glorification even though they are shut out.³¹ Then Paul draws on the "marveled at" of Ps 68:35 (67:36 LXX). He is again applying the language of Yahweh in both psalms' passages to Christ. The Thessalonians will "all" (reassuringly) witness God's repaying their enemies in Christ's coming!³² After all, the Thessalonians have believed the apostolic testimony. This is a passage not primarily about hell but about comforting the persecuted.

"On that day" echoes Isa 2:11, 17. (Second Thessalonians 1 frequently echoes Isa 2 and 66.)³³ The day of the Lord appears to be a still-future event. Mention of it frames this paragraph on reward and punishment, and thus the emphatic position at the end. The late second- and early third-century authors Irenaeus (*Haer.* 4.27.4; 4.28.1–2 [*ANF* 1:500–501]) and Tertullian (*Marc.* 5.6; 5.16) express frustration with those always pointing to Christ's mercy at the expense of God's impending judgment and vengeance.

The causal or parenthetical "that" (*hoti*) clause at the end of the verse reminds the Thessalonians that they believed Paul when he was with them about these things, and they should continue doing so. "Therefore you will also receive this blessing of participation in the Lord's glory because you have believed the gospel that we preached to you."³⁴

Paul again prays in a way that the Thessalonians will overhear (v. 11). He challenges them to continue to believe and endure. God will empower this, making them worthy of his call (see also v. 3). Paul's prayer, given the grammatical connection—whether referring to all of vv. 1–10 or just v. 10—pertains to their present behavior and belief that they may number among the saved. God will enable, complete, and empower them. Origen noted the example of Paul's constant prayer (*Or.* 7).

"Every desire of goodness"—if an objective genitive construction—would be the goodness that drives the Thessalonians' desires, or the desire to do good. A subjective genitive construction would mean every desire that "goodness" prompts in them, desire originating *from* goodness, a strange notion in Paul.³⁵ The emphasis here is on God's fulfilling their every desire to do what is good for others.³⁶ For "work of faith," see 1 Thess 1:3. "Desire of goodness"—is this God's desire or the Thessalonians'?

---

31. Fee, *Thessalonians*, 261.
32. Fee, *Thessalonians*, 262.
33. Witherington, *Thessalonians*, 198.
34. Kim and Bruce, *Thessalonians*, 536–37.
35. Kim and Bruce, *Thessalonians*, 541–42.
36. Fee, *Thessalonians*, 265.

Paul refers to human desire in Rom 10:1; Phil 1:15, and "goodness" is that of humans in Rom 15:14; Gal 5:22; Eph 5:9. Since "work of faith" refers to the Thessalonians' activity, a subjective genitive would indicate the desire stemming from their goodness (even as work from faith).[37] The power for this, nevertheless, is God's (also 1 Thess 1:5; 2 Thess 1:9). God is the one working this and making them worthy of the calling.

Verse 12 gives the reason: The Lord will be glorified in their lives. This glorification is still an eschatological event given the parallels to v. 10. Paul's thanksgivings typically end on a note about the *future* (1 Cor 1:7–8; Phil 1:10; 1 Thess 1:10).[38] Glorification is also typically in the future, for Paul (Rom 5:2; 8:18–19; 1 Cor 15:42–57; Phil 3:20–21; Col 3:4; 2 Thess 2:13–14). Paul again appropriates Isaianic language (Isa 66:5, 7); recall the echoes of Isa 66 earlier in this passage, and he is again applying Yahweh language to Jesus.[39] While Christ is in heaven, absent from earth, his name is thereby glorified on earth.

"In you" parallels v. 10's "in/among his holy ones." Whereas v. 10 was the glorification of Jesus, here in v. 12 believers are included.[40] Jesus's name is glorified by virtue of their good deeds.[41] Again, this is all by the grace of God and the Lord Jesus.

Verse 10 refers to initial faith and v. 12 to perseverance in acts of faith until the end (also 1 Thess 2:12). Christ's own glory becomes the believer's, in a secondary sense (also 1 Cor 2:7).[42]

---

37. Weima, *Thessalonians*, 483.
38. Weima, *Thessalonians*, 485.
39. Fee, *Thessalonians*, 266–67.
40. Weima, *Thessalonians*, 486.
41. Kim and Bruce, *Thessalonians*, 545.
42. Witherington, *Thessalonians*, 201.

9

2 Thessalonians 2:1–17
Stand Firm in View of What Is to Come

Translation

[1] Now WE ASK you brothers and sisters, concerning the coming of our Lord Jesus Christ and our gathering to him, [2] that you not be easily shaken out of [your] mind or upset, whether through a spiritual utterance or through word or through a letter as though from us, how that the day of the Lord has come.

[3] Do not let anyone deceive you in any way, because [the day will not come] unless the rebellion comes first, and the man of lawlessness is revealed, the son of destruction, [4] who opposes and exalts himself over every being called god or object of worship so that he himself sits down in the sanctuary of God, proclaiming of himself that he is God. [5] Do you not remember that when I was still with you I kept telling you these things? [6] And now you know that [there is] a restraint, so that he may be revealed at his own time. [7] For the mystery of lawlessness is already at work, only until the restrainer is out of the way. [8] And then the lawless one will be revealed, whom the Lord Jesus will slay with the breath of his mouth and will abolish by the manifestation of his coming [9] [and] whose own coming will be according to the working of Satan in all power, both signs and wonders of falsehood, [10] and in all deception of wickedness for the ones perishing, because they did not welcome the

love of the truth so as for them to be saved. [11] And for this reason God will send them a working of delusion so that they believe the lie, [12] so that all who did not believe the truth but delighted in wickedness will be condemned.

[13] But as for us, we ought always to thank God for you, brothers and sisters beloved by the Lord, because God chose you as firstfruits for salvation by the sanctification of the Spirit and belief in the truth, [14] for which [salvation] he [God] also called you through our gospel, that you obtain the glory of our Lord Jesus Christ.

[15] So then, brothers and sisters, stand firm and hold onto the traditions that you were taught, whether orally or through our letter.

[16] Now may our Lord Jesus Christ himself and God our Father, who loved us and gave [us] eternal comfort and good hope by [his] grace, [17] comfort your hearts and strengthen you in every good work and word.

Commentary

"[Second Thessalonians 1] introduces the general subject of the present tribulations regarded in an eschatological perspective.... After this preparation chapter two presents the specific problem."[1] Paul had placed the Thessalonians' sufferings within an eschatological perspective (Jesus's "revelation" [1:7], his "coming" [1:10]). After that prior discussion (e.g., 1 Thess 5:1–11)—and not always from Paul himself (the claim in vv. 1–2 by some that the day of the Lord had already come)—the apostle addresses the main concern of the letter. Events are still to come (vv. 3–4), and the day is currently being held back (vv. 5–7). When that day finally comes, they should not be "shaken" (vv. 8–12). Paul thanks God for them, exhorts them, and prays for them, especially that they persevere during this time (vv. 13–17). His concerns are pastoral rather than predictive. Verses 1–12 are nonchronological as Paul alternates between the future and the present. Verse 5–7's events take place *prior* to vv. 3–4's (the appearance of the man of lawlessness) and vv. 9–12's events are *prior* to v. 8's (the destruction of the man of lawlessness).

That Paul words v. 1 as a request (*erotaō*) and not a command signals its importance, as it did in 1 Thess 5:12; note the distinction between appeal (*parakaleō*) and command in Phlm 8–9. Paul reminds them of

---

1. Hartman, "Eschatology," 477–78, here 478.

their new family status ("brothers and sisters" in vv. 1, 13, 15; see also 2 Thess 1:3; 3:1, 6, 13)—which, again, takes precedence over ordinary kin relations.

Second Maccabees 1:27 and 2:7 employ "gathering" (*episynagogēs*) for the Jews after the Babylonian exile (on the concept of a return from exile, see Isa 27:13; 43:4-7; 56:8; Ezek 28:25; Zech 2:6-7 LXX). An eschatological "gathering" is also suggested in T. Naph. 8.3; T. Ash. 7.6-7. Here the word is used in reference to being with the Lord at his coming (the same article governing "coming" and "gathering" [1 Thess 4:13-18; 2 Thess 1:9-12]). Paul alludes to the same event in 1 Thess 4:17; 5:10. (The only other NT use of "gathering" is in Heb 10:25, for worship.)

The Thessalonians are not to be shaken by reports that the day of the Lord has come (v. 2). *Ta enestōta* (perfect tense) may be translated "is present" or "has come" (1 Cor 7:26; Gal 1:4; Heb 9:9). The sense here is "has already come" since "is coming" would not have prompted Paul's correction, and evidence is lacking for taking the verb that way (note 1 Thess 5:2). Paul uses the perfect of this verb for what is present already (Rom 8:38; 1 Cor 3:22; 7:26; Gal 1:4); he does not use "draw near" (*engizō* [Rom 13:12; Phil 2:30]). "Paul would hardly have had to go to these lengths to argue in this way if all that some were saying was that the day of the Lord might be or was near."[2] Perhaps 1 Thess 5:1-11 was misinterpreted as having already happened.

The Thessalonians are not to be shaken by these reports. The notion that the day of the Lord had come (*not* "is at hand" [*ēngiken*] or "near" [*engus*]) requires a (mistaken) spiritualized approach to the coming resurrection, likely since a bodily resurrection of the dead was difficult to grasp or take seriously (Acts 17:16-34), unless the day of the Lord refers to the dark events of dawning eschatological wrath *preceding* Christ's return (1 Thess 5:2-5). The day of the Lord is likely not a literal twenty-four-hour period but the final events of the *present* order before Christ's coming.[3] The Thessalonians' sufferings might have led them to conclude that the day was imminent or had taken place. Eusebius said the persecution under Septimus Severus "disturb[ed] the minds of many"; they concluded that the coming of the antichrist was imminent.[4] Paul stresses in response that this day is still in the future. Augustine noted that the

---

2. Witherington, *Thessalonians*, 214.
3. Wanamaker, *Thessalonians*, 240.
4. Eusebius, *Hist. eccl.* 6.7 (*NPNF*^{2} 1:254).

point is to wait with sincere faith and ardent love for the Lord's coming, whether that coming be near or far away.[5]

Chrysostom took the spirit ("spiritual") as a reference to false prophecy and a forged letter.[6] The reports "as if through us" could have come through a spirit-inspired, false pronouncement, or through reasoned speech, or through written communication, i.e., a spurious epistle. Paul's own authority would trump those three.[7] The Thessalonians in 2 Thess 2:15 are to hold fast to what came to them *directly* by word or letter.[8] Verses 5 and 15 indicate that 1 Thessalonians is not in view: How may one hold fast to his prior teaching (1 Thessalonians) if a false letter is circulating? Paul appears to be unsure where this information is coming from but wants to correct it.

The Thessalonians should not allow themselves to be led astray that the day of the Lord has already come (v. 3). Other events must take place first. The deceit, a strong word, is used to describe the teaching that might have come from well-meaning but misguided congregation members, but erroneous teaching will always deceive.[9]

The apodosis (the main clause) of this conditional sentence must be supplied from what precedes (thus "the day will not come").[10] As for the protasis (the dependent clause of a conditional sentence), the rebellion must come first, a revolt against the one true God (Josh 22:22; Jer 2:19; 1 Macc 2:15). The concept of apostasy from/revolt against God is common in early Judaism (Jub. 23.14–21; 1 En. 91.7; 93.9; 4 Ezra 5.1–12; 14.16–18; Matt 24:12; 2 Tim 3:1–9). The only other NT use of the word is Acts 21:21 where it means apostasy. Jews had already rejected Christ, and Paul nowhere else is anxious about Christ-believing apostasy.[11] He never says in his letters that believers will be deceived. "Rebellion" makes better sense as a translation than "apostasy." These are people who did not welcome the love of the truth (v. 10) but delighted in wickedness.[12]

---

5. Letter 199.15, in Augustine, *Letters*, 367.
6. John Chrysostom, *Homilies on 2 Thessalonians* 3 (on 2:2) (NPNF[1] 13:386).
7. Brookins, *Thessalonians*, 171.
8. On "as though *from* us" (source/authorship) and not "through us" (mediation: content being mediated), see Kim and Bruce, *Thessalonians*, 556–57; contra both Fee, *Thessalonians*, 274–75n21; and Weima, *Thessalonians*, 505–6.
9. Martin, *Thessalonians*, 231.
10. Wanamaker, *Thessalonians*, 244.
11. Kim and Bruce, *Thessalonians*, 564–65.
12. Fee, *Thessalonians*, 281; Weima, *Thessalonians*, 512.

Paul may have already spoken to the Thessalonians about this, and thus there is no further explanation here. "In any way" suggests that Paul does not know exactly what the danger was.[13]

Does the day of the Lord deception refer to one event or a series of events (first rebellion and then man of lawlessness)? Are the events simultaneous or sequential? Note that there is no "then" (*epeita* [1 Cor 15:46; 1 Thess 4:16–17]) or "second" (*deuteron* [1 Cor 12:28]). "First" refers to *both* of these events as prior to Jesus's coming, but Paul does not appear to be laying out a precise timetable. Parallels to "first" without a "second" or "next" are in Rom 1:8; 3:2; 1 Cor 11:18. The use of two separate verbs indicates two separate events: "rebellion" comes first; man of lawlessness revealed. The passage parallels Pss. Sol. 17.11–22 with Pompey's 63 BC campaign as the "lawless one," resulting in Jewish apostasy. Apparently, for Paul, hidden forces of evil will reveal themselves in this rebellion.

The introduction of the man of lawlessness (a human being [Isa 57:4 LXX; Dan 12:10]) in v. 3 forms a striking comparison (*synkrisis*) with Jesus. (1) Both the man of lawlessness and Jesus come; (2) both are hidden from view until their "revealing"/"manifestation" (vv. 7–8); (3) both are powerful figures (vv. 2, 4, 7–9, 11); (4) the man of lawlessness's works are distinguished from—even as he works with—Satan's (v. 9), even as Jesus's works from God the Father's. The man of lawlessness is thus a person, even as is Jesus.[14] This is a rival savior or ruler figure (compare with 1 John 2:18–19), echoing the man of Belial, rendered in the Septuagint with both "lawlessness" (*anomia* [2 Sam 22:4–5 = Ps 18:3–4 (17:4–5 LXX)]) and "apostasy" (*apostasia* [Josh 22:22 LXX; 1 Macc 2:15 LXX]). This could be a future ruler who recapitulates the sins of Antiochus IV Epiphanes (2 Macc 5:11–17; Dan 11:31, 36–37; 12:11; Josephus, *A.J.* 14.4.4 §§69–76), or Pompey (Pss. Sol. 1.19, 28–29; 17.11, 13–20), or Caligula and/or Nero (i.e., an allusion to the emperor cult [Sib. Or. 5.29–34; Josephus, *B.J.* 2.10.1 §§184–185; *A.J.* 18.8.2–9 §§261–309; Philo, *Legat.* 30–43 §§203–346]). Whoever it is, he seems to be leading Jews astray (as in Daniel and Psalms of Solomon). Pagans also influence Jews toward lawlessness in Pss. Sol. 1.8; 2.3.

John Chrysostom identified the man of lawlessness as a human being through whom Satan worked, with the mystery of lawlessness as a type of antichrist.[15] Theodore of Mopsuestia described him as a particular

---

13. Wanamaker, *Thessalonians*, 243.
14. Witherington, *Thessalonians*, 217.
15. John Chrysostom, *Homilies on 2 Thessalonians* 4 (on 2:6–9) (*NPNF*[1] 12:388–89).

man and Satan's tool.[16] For Origen, he is a man who sits in the temple and is perhaps a corporate figure (*Cels.* 2.50). Ambrosiaster said he is a supernatural figure.[17] Behind the "man of lawlessness" or antichrist, explained Thomas Aquinas, is the working of Satan.[18] For the tenth-century Thietland of Einsiedeln, the man of lawlessness is not just the antichrist but also one whom the masses follow.[19] Luther identified this figure not as an emperor or false prophet but the church's papacy (so also Arminius and Bengel).[20] Calvin stressed that apostasy means a departure from God and therefore must take place in the church with the pope.[21] The Roman Catholic exegete Estius at the time of the Reformation understandably responded that the "man of sin" refers to the Roman emperors who had persecuted the church in order to cause people to defect from the faith, and not the pope.[22] The seventeenth-century Matthew Poole also noted the temple in Paul as the church.[23] The pope as the man of lawlessness would become a minority position by the eighteenth century.

"Son of destruction" does not refer to what this figure causes, but rather the intransitive sense of "destruction" (more common in Paul [e.g., Rom 9:22; Phil 1:28; 3:19]) means that this figure's lot is to be destroyed—an understanding confirmed by the destruction of his followers in v. 10.[24] Augustine contrasted this figure's hollow self-glorying with Christ's example of humility.[25]

"Proclaiming himself" (*apodeiknumi* [v. 4]) is used for the "nomination for an office" or the "proclamation of a sovereign upon assuming power" (Philo, *Flacc.* 3 §9). This figure's exalting (lit. "hyper-exalting") himself in the temple of the one true God echoes the king of Dan 11:36 LXX (Antiochus IV Epiphanes); similarly Ezek 28:1–10, esp. v. 2 (the

---

16. Theodore of Mopsuestia, *Commentaries*, 504-7 (Commentary 2.50-51).

17. Ambrosiaster, *Commentaries*, 115.

18. *ST* 1, q. 113, art. 4; obj. 3. On the oneness of the devil and the antichrist in relation to 2 Thess 2, see the lengthy discussion in *ST* 3, q. 9 art. 8: in the antichrist is the fullness of wickedness just as in Christ the fullness of God.

19. Thietland of Einsiedeln, *Second Thessalonians*, 52.

20. Luther, "Pagan Servitude," 306-7; Arminius, *Works*, 2:280-82; Bengel, *Gnomon Novi Testamenti*, 819 ("Papa est quodomodo homo peccati"); Bengel, *Gnomon of the New Testament*, 2:496.

21. Calvin, *Epistles*, 398-99; Calvin, *Institutes* 4.7.25.

22. Estii, *In Omnes Divi Pauli Epistolas*, 2:603-11, here 606-9.

23. Poole, *Commentary*, 3:760.

24. Weima, *Thessalonians*, 515.

25. Augustine, *Tract. Ev. Jo.* 29.8 (*Tractates*, 19-20).

king of Tyre); Isa 14:4–20; 2 Cor 12:7 (a thorn to *keep* Paul from exalting himself). "Man of lawlessness" in v. 3 parallels Dan 12:10. Unlike Daniel, this figure's actions go beyond self-exaltation/deification to outright opposition as an "adversary" (*antikeimenos*). For self-deification (whether as God or *a* god) in the temple of God (*naos* for inner sanctum or "holy of holies"), see Caligula's threatened defiling of the temple with an idolatrous image (Josephus, *A.J.* 18.8.2 §261).

The being calling himself god hopes to supplant the *true* God (1 Cor 8:5–6; Gal 4:8; 1 Thess 1:9).[26] This figure parallels Dan 11:36—a passage prominent in Second Temple eschatological expectations.

The definite article identifies this as a particular temple/sanctuary.[27] A heavenly temple is unlikely since these events are to take place on earth, and Paul does not refer to a heavenly temple elsewhere. Irenaeus took this as a reference to the Jerusalem temple (*Haer.* 4.30.4).

Elsewhere, Paul consistently identifies the temple as the church (1 Cor 3:16–17; 2 Cor 6:16; Eph 2:21).[28] Witherington avers, "Paul nowhere in 1 and 2 Thessalonians refers to the church as 'the Temple of God.'"[29] A united church organization or power structure/base did not exist yet.[30] The largely gentile audience would not have understood "temple of God" as "the church of Christ" without further explanation, especially with the Jerusalem temple still standing, were this a letter from Paul, as seems likely. Paul, however, refers in these letters to his prior instruction. Surely entering a new religious system and departing an old one would render discussion of a temple concept relevant. If so, the doubled article for both nouns may not necessarily point to "the" Jerusalem temple, which had *repeatedly* been desecrated, especially with Antiochus IV Epiphanes's claim to be God. Those who claim reference to the Jerusalem temple (destroyed in AD 70, thus needing to be rebuilt) still claim that Paul is likely using the temple metaphorically for the extent of this figure's lawlessness.[31] The temple reference could be a figurative expres-

26. Weima, *Thessalonians*, 516–17.
27. Best, *Thessalonians*, 286–87.
28. Beale, *Thessalonians*, 207–10.
29. Witherington, *Thessalonians*, 220.
30. Kim and Bruce, *Thessalonians*, 571.
31. For a heavenly temple, see Ps 11:4; Isa 66:1; Mic 1:2; Hab 2:20; 1 En. 14.9–22; 2 Bar. 4.2–6. A human figure would not likely be active there.
Several patristic commentators posited that the Jerusalem temple would be rebuilt, e.g., Barn. 16.4–5; Hippolytus, *Comm. Dan.* 4.49; Souter, *Pelagius' Expositions*, 444 (along with Jewish laws). Ernest Best has this as the Jewish branch broken off in Rom

sion not for the Jerusalem temple's destruction but for the usurpation of God's authority and status.³² Augustine stressed that we cannot be sure in what temple the antichrist sits (*Civ.* 20.19); so also the tenth-century Thietland of Einsiedeln, whether ruins of Solomon's Temple or the church.³³

The man of lawlessness's actions echo the deification of pagan rulers wanting to be treated as a god. Julius Caesar had statues in 46 BC put up with the inscription THEOS EPIPHANES (God manifest). Caligula tried to set up a statue in the Jerusalem temple (Philo, *Legat.* 30–43 §§203–346). Herod Agrippa I in AD 44 received divine honors with Olympic-style games in Caesarea Maritima. He appeared in gold clothing with the sun reflecting on him and mimicked the voice and appearance of a god, only to be struck down (Acts 12:21–23; Josephus, *A.J.* 19.8.2 §§343–347). Claudius (AD 41–54) had a bronze coin issued in nearby Philippi with, on one side, the inscription *colonia augusti iulia philipensis* and, on the other, portraits of Caesar and Octavian with the inscription DIVUS AUG (divine Augustus). Nero in AD 54 had coins minted for Claudius's divine status. Perhaps a future emperor is envisioned in this verse as doing the same.

In an instance of *aposiopesis* (leaving a thought incomplete),³⁴ Paul reminds them in v. 5 of what he ("I") had told them (on more than one occasion) while still with them; he is again emphasizing himself as the primary author of the letter (e.g., 1 Thess 3:4; 4:2, 6, 11; 2 Thess 3:4, 10)—and, again, Paul elsewhere takes the temple as the church. The Thessalonians will simply know what he means regarding the events of vv. 3–4 ("these things") even if the modern reader may not. Second Thessalonians need not be before First Thessalonians; Paul had not really addressed the signs or precursors to the coming in the more general discussion of 1 Thess 4–5. The tone suggests some deterioration in the relationship since 1 Thessalonians.³⁵ Paul does not refer to 1 Thessalonians because 1 Thess 4:13—5:11 was dealing with the fate of *believers*, and even there he referred to prior teaching (5:2, 4–5).

Verse 6 introduces a new subsection, which will not conclude until v. 12, as well as the "restrainer" (a word that does *not* mean "to delay").

11, and thus agreeing with Jub. 23.14–23; 1 En. 91.3–10; 1QpHab II, 1–10 for an apostasy within Judaism (*Thessalonians*, 282–83).

32. With Weima, *Thessalonians*, 522; Brookins, *Thessalonians*, 173.

33. Thietland of Einsiedeln, *Second Thessalonians*, 52.

34. Lausberg, *Handbuch*, 1:438–40 (§§887–888).

35. Malherbe, *Letters to the Thessalonians*, 421.

This figure holds back the man of lawlessness, a comfort for the afflicted Thessalonians. The neuter article with "restrainer" indicates a restraining force, but v. 7 has a masculine participle. Personal agency may be indicated in that the man of lawlessness will not be revealed before "his [the *restrainer's*] time." In the NT the word means "to hold fast" (Luke 8:15; 1 Cor 11:2; 1 Thess 5:21) and "hold back (captive)/restrain" (Rom 1:18; 7:6; Phlm 13).[36] Thus there is the coming of Christ but *also* of the "man of lawlessness," and the "restrainer" is holding back the man of lawlessness's coming in order to prevent the full release of Satan's power and deception. God ultimately controls the timing of events (Isa 13:22; Ezek 12:21–25).

The Greek infinitival clause ("so that he may be revealed") may modify either "the restraint" or "you know." The order would place it with "you know," but that verb already has an object. "Restraint" might have been placed forward for emphasis. The preposition *eis* (so that) could indicate purpose or result. The "he" is likely the person of rebellion since the restraining force in the prior clause is neuter and not masculine as would be expected. The man of lawlessness is the one "revealed" in vv. 3, 8.

In view of its position in the sentence, the "now" likely modifies the restraint and does not indicate that they "now" know this. The temporal markers throughout this passage demonstrate that the day of the Lord has not yet arrived, and the parallel synonym for "now" in v. 7 refers to the restrainer.

Paul appears to have told the Thessalonians about this figure/force already when with them, leaving the verse somewhat opaque for modern readers. The restrainer is at work "now" and until a certain point (vv. 7–8). On the proper times and seasons in God's plan as a motif in apocalyptic literature, see 4 Ezra 4.34–37; 7.74; 2 Bar. 21.8; 48.2–5; 56.2. Paul is comforting the afflicted with the knowledge that God is ultimately the one setting the time, not Satan.

The identity of the restrainer is particularly puzzling.[37] Paul and his gospel preaching are unlikely, since he could very well live to the Lord's return (1 Thess 4–5) and does not envision a time before the return when the gospel gets removed. The restrainer is not the Holy Spirit, since Paul

---

36. For a listing of the papyri attesting to the meaning, see Nicholl, *From Hope to Despair*, 227n10.

37. See the surveys in Metzger, *Katechon*, 15–47; Röcker, *Belial und Katechon*, 422–573.

envisions no greater power, and a withdrawal of the Spirit after Pentecost is not taught elsewhere. God remains at work in 2 Thess 2:11, and the Spirit in 2:13. The church is not a likely restrainer, since the notion of its removal/rapture from the world prior to the end does not emerge until the nineteenth century. Satan is not likely the restrainer of his own ally, the man of lawlessness (vv. 9–10).

Tertullian (*Res.* 24; *Apol.* 32) and Hippolytus (*Comm. Dan.* 4.21) both identified it/him as the Roman emperor or empire—thus the masculine restrainer (v. 7) alternates quite naturally with the neuter restraint (v. 6). The government acts as a restraint against evil (Rom 13:3–4), a "curb . . . on the forces of lawlessness."[38] Daniel 7:24–25 has Israel within its boundaries and under its jurisdiction.[39] However, Paul appears critical of Rome's promise of "peace and security" in 1 Thess 5:2–3. Caligula had *just in AD 40* been trying to set up his image in the Jerusalem temple (note the Antiochus IV allusions, thus a sort of "super-Caligula").[40] "It is difficult to believe that Paul looked to the collapse of Roman rule as a precondition for the final denouement of the present age."[41] Others have broadened the referent to a principle of law and order. The Roman emperor (currently Claudius) and the empire, i.e., as law and order, are viewed *"from the perspective of the need for his [Paul's] mission to all the nations."*[42]

Another candidate for the restrainer is the archangel Michael. Even as the "man of lawlessness" echoes Dan 11:36's end-times enemy and the desecration of the temple in Dan 11:31, Michael plays a major role in Dan 10–12. Paul tends to avoid explicit reference to "angels" in favor of "powers" and "authorities," even as here the name is the entity's *function*.[43] Daniel 12:1–2 describes Michael as "the great prince who protects your people" in a time of unparalleled distress. He is in Jewish literature the most important archangel (1QM XVII, 7; 1 En. 24.6; T. Isaac 2.1; Mart. Isa. 3.15–16; 3 En. 17.3). He blows the trumpet and leads the

---

38. Kim and Bruce, *Thessalonians*, 583. See the defense of this view in Kim, *Paul's Gospel*, 305–9.

39. Witherington, *Thessalonians*, 210.

40. Kim and Bruce, *Thessalonians*, 590, 593.

41. Wanamaker, *Thessalonians*, 250.

42. Kim and Bruce, *Thessalonians*, 591; emphasis in original. Martin Luther thought the restrainer was the secular states ruled by godly princes ("Appeal to the Ruling Class," 417).

43. Hannah, *Michael and Christ*, 122–23, 134; Hannah, "Angelic Restrainer," esp. 44.

charge at the final judgment (Apoc. Mos. [Life of Adam and Eve] 22.1; 1 Thess 4:16—the archangel's signal!). In other texts, Michael is Satan's primary opponent (1 En. 69; 1QM XVII, 5–6; Jude 9; Rev 12:7–9). He defeats Satan in the end in 1QM XIII, 10 (the Prince of Light). Revelation 20:1–3 envisions a powerful angel restraining Satan and chaining him and tossing him into a pit for a thousand years. He "restrains" (*katechon*) Satan in Jewish tradition (*PGM* 4.268–272; 4.2770). He fights Satan in Rev 12:7–9 and casts Satan out of heaven.[44] Michael fights against and restrains evil angels in Dan 10:13, 20–21. He is removed from the scene also in Dan 12:1, which leads to a time of tribulation, and after that the final judgment (12:1–3)—all of which matches 2 Thess 2—and Paul has been alluding in this chapter to Daniel (9:27; 11:31; 12:11).[45] Augustine, and many after him, however, considered the identity of "the restrainer" now obscure (*Civ.* 20.19).[46]

Verse 7's "mystery" (something hidden) is of lawlessness—an epexegetical genitive, "which is"—and that lawlessness is *already* at work prior to the man of lawlessness's arrival. Several Christian thinkers throughout history associated the lawlessness with the Neronic persecution, sometimes viewed as continuing under Diocletian and Julian the Apostate: the ninth-century Haimo of Auxere; Ambrosiaster; Chrysostom.[47] Theodoret of Cyrus (fifth century) took the mystery as *heresies* leading people away from the truth.[48]

The second part of v. 7 appears to include an ellipsis: *monon ho katechōn arti heōs ek mesou genētai* (only until the restrainer is out of the way), with either a supplied "the mystery must continue to work" after *monon* (only) or "will continue to restrain" after *ho katechōn* (the restrainer). The former suggestion accounts for the sequence of thought: it remains a mystery until it is revealed, and only while present is the man of lawlessness "restrained." Verse 7 proves that the neuter restraint of v. 6 is actually a person. Another possibility is that, instead of an ellipsis, "the restrainer" was simply moved forward to *emphasize* the subject; note a

---

44. Nicholl, *From Hope to Despair*, 243–44.

45. See the critique of the Michael hypothesis in Kim, *Paul's Gospel*, 299–302.

46. Also the tenth-century Thietland of Einsiedeln (*Second Thessalonians*, 53); the nineteenth-century Olshausen (*Commentary*, 484, 491–97).

47. Haimo of Auxere, *Exposition*, 25–27; Ambrosiaster, *Commentaries*, 115; John Chrysostom, *Homilies on 2 Thessalonians* 4 (on 2:6–9) (*NPNF*[1] 12:388–89).

48. Theodoret of Cyrus, *Commentaries*, 2:129.

similar shift in word order in Gal 2:10.⁴⁹ The restrainer acts until he is "out of the way," a phrase also used in 1 Cor 5:2; Col 2:14.

"And then" (v. 8) refers to what happens *after* the restrainer is out of the way (not before) and is the same (future) time as in v. 3. "The lawless one" reflects Greek idiomatic usage, whereas "man of lawlessness" is Semitic. *God*, who remains in control, will reveal this hidden figure (i.e., a divine passive construction).

Note the three disclosure words in vv. 8–9: "revealed," "manifestation of [the] coming" of the man of lawlessness, and the "coming" of Christ. "Coming" is the language used for the visitation of the divine emperor to a city.⁵⁰ Similarly, God visits for judgment in the Septuagint (2 Macc 2:21; 3:24).

Slaying "by the breath of his mouth" echoes Isa 11:4 LXX: "And he [the coming prince of the house of David; for Paul, Christ] shall strike . . . with the word of his mouth, and with the breath through his lips he shall do away with the impious" (NETS); also Job 4:9; Ps 33:6 [32:6 LXX] (not destruction but creation); Isa 30:27–28; 1 En. 14.2; 62.2; 84.1; Pss. Sol. 17.24–25; Wis 11:19–20. Paul discusses, out of order, his end (v. 8) before his coming (v. 9). The breath of his mouth recalls the powerful Spirit creating the universe and bringing order from chaos in Gen 1:2–3. God's judgment will be by a mere word rather than a war (the word acting as the sword [Rev 19:21] or a simple fire from heaven [Rev 20:7–10]).

"Abolish," i.e., destroy, creates a parallelism between the first ("slay") and second halves of the verse (future indicative verb ["will slay/abolish"], article and instrumental dative noun ["with the breath/by the manifestation"], article and defining genitive noun ["of the mouth/of the coming"], and possessive third-person plural pronoun ["his"]), doubly about death.⁵¹ "Manifestation" conveys better the *suddenness* of the coming, or perhaps the splendor of his appearance; this is the *means* by which the enemy is destroyed.⁵² God will allow the man of lawlessness to be revealed, and then Jesus will destroy him.

The man of lawlessness's coming (v. 9) parallels/imitates Christ's "coming" with every [kind of] power, both signs and wonders (unlike a genuine apostle [2 Cor 12:12]).⁵³ This is not a triad, since "power" is in

---

49. Wanamaker, *Thessalonians*, 256; Weima, *Thessalonians*, 531.
50. Also of Isis manifesting herself to a person (Diodorus Siculus, *Bib. hist.* 1.25).
51. Weima, *Thessalonians*, 536.
52. Weima, *Thessalonians*, 537.
53. On the translation, see Fee, *Thessalonians*, 293.

the plural and the other nouns in the singular. "Signs and wonders" is a frequent pairing (e.g., Exod 7:3; Deut 4:34; 6:22; Isa 8:18; Rom 15:19). Consequently, "all" modifies only the first noun, which matches in gender, number, and case. Satan is therefore endowing the man of lawlessness with "all power," as God did Christ. Both the man of lawlessness and Christ have their "comings," both exert supernatural power, the man of lawlessness works by Satan's power whereas Christ works by the true God's, and both are revealed. One stands for the truth and the other the lie, with no middle ground.

Caligula could be, for Paul, a type of the man of lawlessness to come. Athanasius interpreted the verse as fulfilled in his own day with the emperor Constantius, who had supported Arianism (*H. Ar.* 77).

Note the juridical language in the passage ("be judged," truth, lie). The eschatological judgment will reverse this situation and any wrong verdicts in human courts of affairs.

Paul shifts in v. 10 from the man of lawlessness to the people being deceived ("deception" [Eph 4:22; Col 2:8]). "The ones perishing" (1 Cor 1:18; 2 Cor 2:15; 4:3) are likely deceived by the satanic miracles. They did not welcome "the love of the truth" but preferred deceit and error. "Truth" is synonymous with the gospel (2 Cor 4:2; 13:8; Gal 2:5, 14; 5:7; Eph 1:13; Col 1:5–6) and the Christian faith (Eph 4:21; 6:14; 1 Tim 2:4, 7; 3:15; 4:3; 6:5; 2 Tim 2:15, 18, 25; 3:7, 8; 4:4; Titus 1:14). "The lawless man . . . will take his adherents to perdition with him."[54]

Paul is back from the future in v. 11 with an uncharacteristic paratactic "and," thereby linking to vv. 6 and 8. The perishing refuse to love God's truth, and so God sends a powerful delusion. Is this *prior to* the working of the man of lawlessness, thus enabling that man's work to succeed? Or does God's deception *consist in* the working of the man of lawlessness? The present tense verb ("sends") may support the former: God is sending deception *now* on those rejecting the truth, i.e., the Thessalonian non–Christ believers.[55] The present tense, however, is not conclusive since it is also used for the hidden man of lawlessness's future coming in v. 9. Verses 7–12 are more likely in the future since vv. 1–2 are about future events *before* the day of the Lord, which have not yet happened.

Paul describes *both* the man of lawlessness and God as "working" deceit/delusion. Satan and God are thus placed in parallel. For a spirit of

---

54. Kim and Bruce, *Thessalonians*, 609.
55. Weima, *Thessalonians*, 542–44.

deceit sent by God, see 1QS III, 18–26, esp. 18–19. The whole series of events is according to God's plan, and so God's deception refers to the same activity as the man of lawlessness (Rom 1:18–32; 11:7–10). Thus the present tense of vv. 10–12 is from the perspective of the future when the man of lawlessness is at work, and there *will be* some who *are* perishing because they did not previously believe.[56]

Calvin noted the long tradition of taking this as a warning about those professing Christ apostasizing near the end at the time of the antichrist, "the future dispersion of the church" when the church "must be reduced to a ghastly and horrifying state of ruin, before its full restoration is achieved"—in an immediate context preceding Calvin's turn to the errors of the "Romanists."[57]

As a result, all not believing the truth will be judged (v. 12). God sends a delusion to prevent them from seeing and hearing (as in Isa 29:10), thus confirming them in their choice (Rom 1:28), the god of this age blinding minds (2 Cor 4:4). For a climax of wickedness in the last days, see Pss. Sol. 17.22–29. The increase of evil is much like the frog in the kettle of water that is being heated gradually. Paul is reinforcing the sense that separation is necessary from a world that rejects the truth.[58] The condemnation in this verse revisits the penalty for the wicked's actions in 2 Thess 1:6, 9.

Athanasius pointed out that not knowing when the end will occur is good lest people ignore the present time and focus only on themselves (*C. Ar.* 3.49–50). Similarly, God is silent about the time of each individual's death so that people will advance forward day by day toward the end.

"But as for us" (v. 13)—this further contrast of the two groups is to comfort believers as those destined for salvation. Paul mentions why he ought to thank God for them in prayer. This verse is identical to 2 Thess 1:3, but whereas 1:3 involved thanksgiving for their virtues, here it is for God's activity in their lives, quite unlike those perishing and refusing the truth in v. 10. Tatian stressed in the second century that thanks are *due* God from those who believe (*Or. Graec.* 20 [*ANF* 2:73]).

"Beloved by the Lord" echoes Moses's blessing on the tribe of Benjamin (Deut 7:7–8; 33:12 LXX), and Paul was a Benjaminite (Rom 11:1; Phil 3:5). This subtle Pauline nuance militates for authenticity.[59] The lan-

---

56. Brookins, *Thessalonians*, 178–79.
57. Calvin, *Epistles*, 398–99.
58. Wanamaker, *Thessalonians*, 263.
59. Fee, *Thessalonians*, 299n95.

guage also echoes the love of the Lord for Israel, now applied to Christ believers (Isa 44:2; Jer 11:15; 12:7 LXX).

Note the proto-Trinitarian "beloved by the Lord" (instead of the usual "God"), whom "God chose" and the Spirit sanctified.[60] Had Paul meant by "Lord" God and not Christ, he could have said "beloved by him, because he chose you" as opposed to *distinguishing* "Lord" from the following "God."[61]

On God's choosing/election, see also 1 Thess 1:2–4; 2:12; 3:3; 4:7; 5:9, 24. The choice of Greek word for "choose" (*haireō* for "elect/choose/take/prefer"; a NT *hapax* in that sense) may be influenced by Deut 26:17–18 LXX where God chooses Israel, in which case God is now choosing gentiles! The choice of God has evoked discussion through the centuries. Thomas Aquinas wrote: "[God] gives certain goods to some men, which He does not give to others."[62] This merciful election is despite a person's unworthiness.[63] Augustine stressed that God chooses some and saves them by changing their wills.[64] "Their purpose is not their own but God's."[65] Luther wrote against Erasmus in *The Bondage of the Will* that God's choice and action are what saves; similarly Calvin.[66] Or with the seventeenth-century Puritan Thomas Watson on this verse: "We may read of God's predestinating love in the work of grace in our heart."[67]

"Firstfruits" (Deut 26:18; Rom 8:23; 11:16; 16:5; 1 Cor 15:20, 23; 16:15) lacks the Greek article (anarthrous) and is indefinite: they are *not* the first believers in Macedonia (see 1 Thess 2:2 and Philippi).[68] They are the firstfruits *in Thessalonica*. The Thessalonians are part of a great eschatological harvest![69] They are, however, firstfruits in the Macedonian capital.[70]

Paul never uses elsewhere in his letters the variant (*ap' archēs*) for "from the beginning of time" (1 Cor 2:7; Eph 1:4; Col 1:26). *Archē* means

---

60. Fee, *Thessalonians*, 300.
61. Weima, *Thessalonians*, 547.
62. *ST* 1, q. 23, art. 5; also art. 3.
63. *ST* 1, q. 23, art. 7, reply to obj. 3.
64. Augustine, *Enchir.* 98.
65. Augustine, *Corrept.* 14.
66. Calvin, *Institutes* 3.21–22.
67. Watson, *Practical Divinity*, 150.
68. Brookins, *Thessalonians*, 181.
69. Weima, *Thessalonians*, 551.
70. Kim and Bruce, *Thessalonians*, 620.

normally "ruler" or "authority" in Paul (Rom 8:38; 1 Cor 15:24).[71] God completes their salvation through the sanctifying work of the Spirit.

The Holy Spirit or the human spirit (2 Cor 7:1; 1 Thess 5:23) could be in view. Note, however, the Spirit's sanctifying activity (Rom 15:16; 1 Cor 6:11–12; 1 Thess 1:4–5; 4:7–8). Since the phrase modifies "God chose you as firstfruits for salvation" (on the day of the Lord), it completes a Trinitarian complex of activity, as the fourth-century Ambrose of Milan recognized.[72]

On "belief," see 2 Thess 1:10 (also 1:3–4, 11). This is the corresponding human response to divine activity and not a subjective genitive for the truth creating faith—thus, the phrase is "faith/belief in the truth."

"For which" (v. 14) likely refers to the whole prior clause in v. 13, "for salvation by sanctification of the Spirit and belief in the truth." God chose them (v. 13) and realized it through the gospel proclamation.[73] God's word thus bears the power to create faith.

Ultimately, it is God who calls through Paul and his coworkers' preaching (1 Thess 1:5; 2:12; 5:24). "Gospel" does not refer to written Gospels until Irenaeus (*Haer.* 3.1.1 [*ANF* 1:414]). Here it is through the oral proclamation that the Thessalonians would one day obtain the glory of Christ. "Obtaining glory" is a Greco-Roman motif in which honor is gained through public works or exploits of war. It is used here to parallel 2 Thess 1:11–12's works of faith bringing glory to the name of the Lord in their salvation.[74] That Paul does not warn his hearers in vv. 13–14 further reassures them of the certainty of their election and salvation.[75]

The resumptive conclusion "orally or through our letter" (v. 15) links to v. 2, and thus this paragraph should not be severed from vv. 1–12.[76] The main verb means to *continue* to "stand firm" through ongoing effort and persistence (1 Cor 16:13; Phil 1:27; 1 Thess 3:8).

Unlike in 2 Thess 2:2, Paul does not mention spirit-inspired prophecy—perhaps an indication that false prophecy had been the source for

---

71. In favor of the variant, see Wanamaker, *Thessalonians*, 266; but see Weima, *Thessalonians*, 550–51.

72. Ambrose, *On the Holy Spirit* 3.4.27–28 (*NPNF*[2] 10:139).

73. Wanamaker, *Thessalonians*, 267; Fee, *Thessalonians*, 303–4.

74. Diodorus Siculus, *Bib. hist.* 9.1.3; 11.39.2; 11.41.3; 15.29.2; "The Education of Children," in Plutarch, *Mor.* 12C; Polybius, *Hist.* 20.4.2; Josephus, *A.J.* 12.8.6 §350; Brookins, *Thessalonians*, 182; Rom 5:2; 8:17–18; Phil 3:21; 1 Thess 2:12; 5:9–10; 2 Tim 2:10.

75. Kim and Bruce, *Thessalonians*, 618, 627.

76. Fee, *Thessalonians*, 297.

the claim that the day of the Lord had come and had led them astray from what Paul himself had previously taught.[77] They are to beware the lawless man's deceptions. The Thessalonians are to test what they receive. "Hold onto," a more forceful emphasis, is elsewhere in the Pauline corpus only in Col 2:19.

Passing on traditions, whether by apostolic letter or mouth, recalls also 1 Thess 4:1. Similar to Rom 16:17 and Gal 1:8, the Thessalonians are to maintain the traditions they were taught by *Paul*, even as philosophers handed down to students their teachings.[78] The second-century Clement of Alexandria emphasized the divine origin of these traditions, since humans are otherwise incapable of uttering anything true about God (*Strom.* 6.18 [*ANF* 2:519]).

The prayer in v. 16 is well placed since Paul has been exhorting the Thessalonians and will again in the next chapter. The prayer is similar to that in 1 Thess 3:11–13.[79] Paul concludes a chapter intended to comfort with "*eternal* comfort," thus preparing his hearers for a life of good works/words.

The Lord Jesus and God the Father, again, act together, with an emphatic "the Lord *himself*" (1 Thess 3:11; 5:23; 2 Thess 3:16). Christ is mentioned before God, as in 2 Cor 13:13 and Gal 1:1, but here the ordering may be a function of God as the subject of the following participial clause (but perhaps not to the exclusion of Jesus). John Calvin remarked on the divine Christology of this verse.[80]

The aorist tense of "loved" may allude to a past event such as the death of Christ (Gal 1:4; 2:20; Eph 5:2), but "gave" is also aorist. The aorist is more likely final, simply expressing the current state.[81] God "comforts," the same word in Rom 15:5; 2 Cor 1:3. In epitaphs, the "good hope" was for the afterlife, and here for the Thessalonians' future (again, "*eternal* comfort") (see Julian, *Ep.* 20.452C; author's translation).[82] On "good hope" as potentially a secular expression, see Josephus, *A.J.* 1.20.1 §325; 5.6.5 §222; 8.8.1 §214; 13.6.4 §201; 14.6.1 §96. What the Thessalonians had been looking for in their world is found in the eternal comfort of the Christ movement.

77. Weima, *Thessalonians*, 558–59.
78. For references, see Brookins, *Thessalonians*, 183.
79. See the comparison in Fee, *Thessalonians*, 307–8.
80. Calvin, *Epistles*, 412.
81. Witherington, *Thessalonians*, 238–39.
82. Witherington, *Thessalonians*, 239.

God gives comfort/encouragement to their (anxious) hearts (v. 17), which also grounds and establishes them in good works and speech, and Paul here prays that this be so. "Good" is repeated for emphasis (on work and word, see also Rom 15:18; Col 3:17). God-given hope should spur them to action and godly behavior. They are to say and do all that is good (2 Cor 9:8), a foundation for 2 Thess 3:6–15. The prayers of 2:16–17 therefore parallel 3:11–13, with "strengthen" again in 3:3. "Every good work and word" would therefore apply to the idle of 3:6–15, who are apparently *not* active in every good work and word.

10

2 Thessalonians 3:1–18
Faithfulness and Against the Disorderly; Closing

Translation

[1] As FOR OTHER matters, pray for us, brothers and sisters, that the word of the Lord may speed along and be honored, just as [it is] also with you, [2] also that we may be rescued from the wicked and evil people, since not everyone [has] faith. [3] But faithful is the Lord, who will strengthen and will guard you from the evil one. [4] And we have been confident in the Lord concerning you, that you are doing and will do the things we are commanding you. [5] May the Lord direct your hearts to the love of God and [to] the endurance of Christ.

[6] Now we are commanding you, brothers and sisters, in the name of [our] Lord Jesus Christ to keep away from every brother or sister continuing to walk in a disorderly manner and not according to the tradition that they received from us. [7] For you yourselves know how it is necessary to imitate us, because we were not disorderly among you, [8] nor did we eat bread from anyone free of charge, but rather we were working with labor and toil night and day in order not to burden any of you. [9] Not that we do not have a right [to be supported], but [we worked] in order that we might present ourselves to you as an example in order for you to imitate us. [10] For, indeed, when we were with you, we were commanding you that if anyone does not want to work, let him not eat.

[11] For we hear that there are some among you walking in a disorderly manner, not working but rather being busybodies. [12] But such people we are commanding and exhorting in the Lord Jesus Christ that they eat their own bread by working with quietness. [13] But as for you, brothers and sisters, do not grow weary in doing good. [14] But if anyone does not obey our instruction through this letter, take note of this person, so as not to associate with him in order to shame [the person]. [15] And yet do not consider him as an enemy, but admonish him as a brother.

[16] Now may the Lord of peace himself give you peace at all times and in every way. The Lord be with you all.

[17] The greeting is by my own hand—Paul's, which is a sign in every letter; I write this way.

[18] The grace of our Lord Jesus Christ be with you all.

Commentary

"As for other matters" (v. 1) turns to what remains/finally (as in 2 Cor 13:11; Phil 4:8); often it is transitional: furthermore (e.g., Phil 3:1). The request for the brothers and sisters' prayers parallels 1 Thess 5:25 (also Rom 15:30–32; Phil 1:19; Col 4:3–4; Phlm 22). Paul will pray for them in v. 5, thus a mutual obligation.[1] Pelagius viewed Paul's request for prayer as an expression of humility; so also the tenth-century Thietland of Einsiedeln.[2] Calvin remarked on Paul's robust life of prayer.[3] Augustine reflected on v. 1:

> Let us offer prayers for one another; let my prayers be offered for you, and yours for me. And, brethren, do not think that you need my prayers, but that I have no need of yours. We have mutual need of one another's prayers, for those reciprocal prayers are enkindled by charity and—like a sacrifice offered on the altar of piety—are fragrant and pleasing to the Lord. If the Apostles used to ask for prayers on their own behalf, how much more does it behoove me to do so? For I am far from being their equal, although I long to follow their footsteps as closely as

---

1. So John Chrysostom, *Homilies on 2 Thessalonians* 4 (on 3:1) (NPNF[1] 12:390).

2. Souter, *Pelagius' Expositions*, 447; Thietland of Einsiedeln, *Second Thessalonians*, 64.

3. Calvin, *Epistles*, 413.

possible; but I have neither the wisdom to know nor the rashness to say what progress I have made.[4]

For the prayer that the word of the Lord speed along, note the echo of Ps 147:15 (147:4 LXX), but Paul uses a different word for running and does not include the reference to running "speedily," as in 1 Thess 1:8. Paul prays for the spread and reception of the word (also Col 4:3)—just as the word has been received by the Thessalonians themselves. The ninth-century Haimo of Auxere anticipated this word creating good works.[5]

Echoes reverberate of the Isthmian games farther south at Corinth with runners, judges, and the victor's crown (1 Cor 9:24–27; Gal 2:2; 5:7; Phil 2:16). The prayer for the swift spread of the word may reflect the impending events outlined in 2 Thess 2.

Paul also asks (v. 2) that they pray he be delivered from wicked people who are not of the faith and who are standing in the way of the word of the Lord's free course (bad and evil [1 Cor 5:8–13]). Clement of Alexandria would repeat this prayer,[6] as would John Chrysostom.[7] Thus, the world is divided into the ungodly and the holy, explained Augustine.[8] Calvin warned of treacherous people who only bear the name of Christian or Jew and who stand against the Word.[9]

Paul could be writing these words when he was on trial at Corinth before Gallio in AD 51 or 52 (Acts 18:12–17). A similar request is in Rom 15:30–31; 2 Cor 1:8–11 (deliverance from people opposing the gospel), 11:23–25 (suffering at the hands of opponents). The verse echoes the wicked persecutor in Scripture (Ps 140:1 [139:2 LXX]; Isa 25:4 LXX). The passive "delivered" points to God's activity against "wicked" or perverse (lit. "out of place" [*atopos*]) people (Job 27:6; 34:12; 36:21 LXX; Luke 23:41; Acts 25:5; Philo, *Leg.* 3.17 §53). Paul faced opposition since not all obeyed the gospel (Rom 10:16); note the persecution in 2 Thess 1:5–10; 2:9–12.

Paul's reference to faith naturally leads to God's faithfulness (v. 3). Verses 3–4 prepare for the exhortations and concern about "doing" in vv. 6–13. Not all have faith (v. 3), but the Lord is faithful—a wordplay

---

4. Sermon 13.10, in Augustine, *Commentary on the Lord's Sermon*, 354–55.
5. Haimo of Auxere, *Exposition*, 31.
6. Clement of Alexandria, *Strom.* 5.3 (ANF 2:448).
7. John Chrysostom, *Homilies on 2 Thessalonians* 4 (on 3:2) (NPNF¹ 12:390–92).
8. Augustine, *Catech.* 19.31.
9. Calvin, *Epistles*, 413.

(Deut 7:9 [the same point about the Lord's faithfulness]; 32:4; Ps 145:13 [144:13 LXX]; Isa 49:7; 1 Thess 5:24). *God* is faithful (1 Cor 1:9; 10:13; 2 Cor 1:18; 1 Thess 5:24). The same contrast between human unfaithfulness/unbelief and God's faithfulness is in Rom 3:3-4. The "Lord" is consistently Jesus, thus 2 Thess 2:14, 16, a few verses before; 3:6; also 1 Cor 8:6. Paul is emphasizing in this letter the actions of the Lord (2 Thess 2:13; 3:16).

The Lord will guard them from the evil one (Pss 12:7 [11:8 LXX]; 121:7 [120:7 LXX]). A masculine "evil one" is more likely than the neuter "evil," since Paul has already referred to evil people from whom the Thessalonians need to be rescued in v. 2, and a contrast with the Lord works better if a reference to the evil one. Satan's role is heightened in the Thessalonian correspondence (1 Thess 2:18; 3:5; 2 Thess 2:9). With the "evil one" connected to the evil people of v. 2, the wicked are unwitting agents of the evil one. Paul does not normally use "evil" for Satan (Satan [1 Thess 2:18; 2 Thess 2:9], tempter [1 Thess 3:5]). Although uncommon in Second Temple Judaism (1 En. 69.15), the early Christians would use "the evil one" for Satan (Matt 13:19; Eph 6:16; 1 John 2:13-14; 5:18-19). Paul uses it for evil in general (Rom 12:9; 1 Thess 5:22) but in the neuter. The Lord (Jesus) is contrasted in vv. 3-5 with the evil one, even as Jesus was pitted against the man of lawlessness in 2 Thess 2:3-12.

Whereas in 1 Thess 3:13 and 2 Thess 2:17 the converts' *hearts* were to be established/strengthened, here it is the converts themselves. Paul uses "guard" differently in Rom 2:26 and Gal 6:13 for keeping the law. The Lord will strengthen them for their labors, despite the opposition.

Paul is *confident* the Lord will help them (v. 4), a confidence formula as in Rom 14:14; 2 Cor 2:3; Gal 5:10; Phil 2:24; Phlm 21. Paul indirectly commands them by referring to what they are already doing; see 1 Thess 4:11's command (also 1 Thess 4:6, 10, 12) but here in the stronger sense of a given command. Again, the confidence is in what the *Lord* is doing. All this could be in reference to the request for prayer in 2 Thess 3:1-2 since nothing would indicate a more comprehensive obedience of the traditions yet.

Verse 5 summarizes the prior chapters and prepares for the charge in vv. 6-15. The Lord (still Christ) is at work guiding and directing their hearts. On directing prayer, see the only other instance of this word in the Pauline corpus in 1 Thess 3:11: "make straight" in that context. Paul is employing a Septuagintalism that appears in 1 Chr 29:18; 2 Chr 12:14; 19:3; 20:33; 30:19; Ps 78:8 (77:8 LXX); Prov 21:2; Sir 49:3; 51:20.

Note the juxtaposition of God and Christ in a high Christology again. "The love of God and the endurance of Christ"—taking the expressions as parallel—could both be objective or subjective genitives. The question is whether they express divine activity or human emulation of God and Christ's activity. God's own love is likely in view of Rom 5:5; 8:32; 2 Cor 13:13, and this love is at work in their hearts. They are to persevere like Christ since God has enabled this (Rom 15:4–5 vs. Jas 5:11). The genitive expressions are thus *delightfully ambiguous*, pointing both to God's activity and to the human response as the Thessalonians become imitators (similarly 1 Thess 1:6). The verse is therefore exhortative.[10]

On this translation of "endurance," see 1 Thess 1:3 (love and endurance) and 2 Thess 1:4 (your endurance). Again, this is not just emulating Christ but is also what Christ himself imparts.[11]

A distinct subunit begins in v. 6 with "commanding" (2 Thess 3:4, 6, 10, 12), an uncommon word in Paul (1 Cor 7:10; 11:17; 1 Thess 4:11; 1 Tim 1:3; 4:11; 5:7; 6:13, 17), and the word binds the section together, with v. 16's peace benediction starting a new unit. The command comes with the authority of Jesus (1 Cor 1:10; 5:4; 7:10; 1 Thess 4:2).[12] To disobey Paul would be to disobey the Lord (2 Thess 3:4). Paul begins here by addressing those living properly. The repeated commands suggest that the situation has grown worse since 1 Thessalonians.

Paul admonishes the entire assembly to shun/keep away from those acting in a disorderly or undisciplined way (note the *command* in 1 Thess 5:14)—thus signaling to the brother or sister, while *still* a brother or sister, that the conduct is unacceptable (avoiding those bringing contrary teaching [Rom 16:17–20]; the only other use in the middle, but with an unclear sense [2 Cor 8:20]; "avoiding" [Mal 2:5 LXX]). Paul has already warned of such people in 1 Thess 4:9–12, but the tone here is more severe. In the Thessalonian family setting, a pariah status would be an existential threat, cutting one off socially and economically.[13]

"Disorderly" is military language for insubordination (Xenophon, *Cyr.* 7.2.6; Demosthenes, *3 Olynth.* 11). These people are not just idle but also out of order. They are not good soldiers for the Lord. *How* they are disorderly and idle is unclear, whether in evangelism, reliance on

---

10. Boring, *Thessalonians*, 294.

11. Witherington, *Thessalonians*, 244.

12. See also Ignatius, *Pol.* 5; John Chrysostom, *Homilies on 2 Thessalonians* 5 (on 3:6) (NPNF[1] 12:393–94).

13. Green, *Thessalonians*, 345; Weima, *Thessalonians*, 605.

patrons, expectation of an imminent end, or a sense of entitlement to the support the apostles enjoyed. "Disorderly" carries the senses of both idle and disruptive here. Paul had already dealt with such people during his initial visit and then in his first letter (1 Thess 4:11–12; 5:14). To disobey Paul is to be "disorderly," i.e., *out of line* with the apostolic teaching. The Thessalonians are to keep their distance from such a person. Chrysostom stressed that believers are to withdraw from those who hold opinions contrary to the doctrine.[14]

A teacher was expected to model his teaching (v. 7).[15] The "tradition" (v. 6, and v. 7's "for") they are to adhere to was not just teaching but also the apostolic example (1 Cor 7:7–9; Gal 4:12–20; Phil 1:30; 3:17; 4:9; 1 Thess 1:6; 2:14). Paul is not asking of them what he was not already himself doing (1 Cor 4:16; 11:1) and what they already know (1 Thess 2:1; 3:3; 4:2; 5:2).

Paul himself worked night and day (v. 8; 2 Cor 11:7–9; 1 Thess 2:9). The broken grammatical construction here is unlikely had a pseudonymous author been dependent on 1 Thess 2:9.[16] Paul asks them to imitate him (likewise 1 Cor 4:16; 11:1; Phil 4:9). He did not take anything for free. He did not eat bread without the sweat of his brow (Gen 3:19 LXX) or without labor and toil (2 Cor 11:27; 1 Thess 2:9) in order not to burden them (placing no obstacle to the gospel [1 Cor 9:12]). John Cassian in the early fifth century noted Paul's example.[17] He was working, but some at Thessalonica were not (2 Thess 3:11); he did not eat anyone's bread freely (3:12), but they did; "we" did not act disruptively (3:7), but they did (3:11). On v. 8 and working, Basil the Great warned: "We have reason to fear, therefore, lest, perchance, on the day of judgment this fault also may be alleged against us, since he who has endowed us with the ability to work demands that our labor be proportioned to our capacity."[18]

Paul had a right to be supported (v. 9; also 1 Cor 9:3–18, esp. 9:14–15; 2 Cor 11:7–15), but he did not exercise that right or authority while ministering among them. He *still* worked! Against those refusing to work (v. 10), he reminds the Thessalonians of his teaching while with them that they are not to eat if they do not work.[19] Paul says much the same

---

14. John Chrysostom, *Homily on Romans* 32 (on 16:17–18) (NPNF[1] 11:559–60).
15. E.g., Cicero, *De or.* 2.20–23 §§87–97; Seneca, *Ep.* 6.5–6.
16. Wanamaker, *Thessalonians*, 284.
17. Cassian, *Institutes* 10.8–13 (NPNF[2] 11:269–71).
18. Basil of Caesarea, "Long Rules," 307.
19. On working: Gen 3:17–19; Prov 6:6–11; 10:4; 12:11; Matt 10:10; 1 Cor 9:1–14;

in 1 Thess 2:9–12; 3:5; 4:9–12; 5:12–22. Calvin insisted that humanity was created to do work.[20] Or with the seventeenth- to eighteenth-century Matthew Henry: "Such as could work, and would not, are not to be maintained in idleness.... We must never... tire in our work. It will be time enough to rest when we come to heaven."[21]

Rome helped their poor with the grain dole, but not all the cities in the empire had such a program. The poor would hire themselves out as day laborers, drawing on their skill or trade. The Thessalonians are to work and not to rely on patrons. The first-century Didache warned of those overextending hospitality beyond three days as false prophets (11:3–12). A person living in idleness is simply not a Christian (12:3–5); so also Tertullian (*Idol.* 5).

The present tense in v. 11 signals a shift to the current situation at Thessalonica. The disorderly are to be busy, and not busybodies (meddlers)—thus the play on words in the Greek. They are to mind their own business and work. Popular philosophers, often busybodies, would mooch off patrons (Lucian, *Icar.* 20; Dio Chrysostom, *Lib.* 80.1). Street-preaching Cynics would demand charity at people's homes.[22] Philosophers were sensitive to the charge. Such busybodies cannot endure quietness and prefer to meddle in others' affairs.[23] The church is to discipline this minority ("some").

Paul does not typically name offenders, and thus "such people" in v. 12 (also 1 Cor 5:1; 2 Cor 2:5; 10:2, 12; Gal 1:7; 2:12). They are to be quiet, Paul commands, *not* in the sense of silence but rather by refraining from interfering as *busybodies* (v. 11) and by working for their food (1 Thess 4:11; 1 Tim 2:2).

Paul returns to the majority at Thessalonica ("but as for you" [v. 13]) and urges them not to grow weary in their labors for good (Matt 12:12; Luke 6:27; Acts 10:33; Gal 6:9 [almost identical but general in application, whereas a more specific application in 2 Thess 3:13]; Phil 4:14; 1 Thess 5:15, 21; 2 Thess 1:11; 2:17).

---

2 Cor 11:7–11; Ps.-Phoc. 153–154; Dio Chrysostom, *Ven.* 7.103–153; Letter 83.7, in Cyril of Alexandria, *Letters*; Augustine, *Op. mon.* 1, 4, followed by Thomas Aquinas—at length, in reference to the Thessalonian correspondence (ST 2.2, q. 187, art. 3 obj. 1–2, reply to obj. 5).

20. Calvin, *Epistles*, 418.

21. Henry, *Concise Commentary*, 936.

22. Diogenes of Sinope, epistles 10, 34, 37, in Malherbe, *Cynic Epistles*, 103–5, 143–44, 155–59.

23. "On Being a Busybody," in Plutarch, *Mor.* 518E; Epictetus, *Diatr.* 3.22.97.

2 THESSALONIANS 3:1–18

They are to mark those not obeying Paul's instructions (v. 14), as he had admonished in 2 Thess 3:6. On *logos* as instruction or a rule of conduct, see Rom 13:9; Gal 5:14.[24] Here Paul is referring specifically to his command to work and not to the entire letter. The disobedient are to be noted (see the similar command in Rom 16:17); thus he makes discipline a corporate responsibility. The church is to shun and shame these people, but not as enemies.

Honor-shame conventions dominated the first-century Mediterranean world of limited goods. Not associating with the disciplined would, at the least, entail not eating with them (1 Cor 5:9–11). Not being invited to meals would also prevent mooching off patrons and hopefully shame the individual to repent of such actions (on shaming/repentance, 1 Cor 4:14; 6:5; 2 Cor 2:6–7; 7:10; Titus 2:8). The shunned is to eat alone. Again, the hope is restoration (as also for the discipline in 1 Cor 5:5; Gal 6:1). Tertullian wrote: "Associate not with him, that he may feel awed, not regarding (him) as an enemy, but rebuking him as a brother" (*Pud.* 13 [*ANF* 4:87]); so also John Chrysostom—since, by withdrawing, he (the erring brother) "will quickly be lost if he is not admitted to freedom of conversation."[25] Chrysostom commented elsewhere that to cut off the disobedient is really an act of love for that person's good and, again, not as an enemy.[26] The early second-century Shepherd of Hermas (Mand. 2.4.1 [*ANF* 2:22]) said of an adulterer: "Withdraw from him and cease to live with him, otherwise you are a sharer in his sin." Augustine said that one is to have no company with those who are disobedient of the Word, but out of love.[27] Excommunication, he wrote elsewhere, drives out wickedness (*Fid. op.* 2–3, in reference to 1 Cor 5:5). For the tenth-century Thietland of Einsiedeln, those who do not obey and are hostile to the evangelical/apostolic teaching are to be avoided.[28] Calvin: Those who disobey God's word are to be excommunicated and avoided in order to prevent the disease from infecting others.[29] Such an approach to discipline is at odds with permissiveness, which is, ironically, anything but an expression of love. Sin and error must always be addressed.

---

24. Wanamaker, *Thessalonians*, 288–89.
25. John Chrysostom, *Homilies on 2 Thessalonians* 5 (on 3:14) (*NPNF*[1] 13:395).
26. John Chrysostom, *Homilies on 1 Corinthians* 33 (on 13:8) (*NPNF*[1] 12:200–201).
27. Augustine, *Serm.* 14.3.
28. Thietland of Einsiedeln, *Second Thessalonians*, 71.
29. Calvin, *Epistles*, 421; Calvin, *Institutes* 4.12.5.

The Thessalonians are not to give up on the erring (v. 15). Withdrawal is not to be a complete avoidance that would prevent further admonishment. The disciplined remains a "brother or sister"! On admonishing family members, see 1 Cor 4:14. Admonition and rebuke were thought effective in producing repentance and shame ("On Moral Virtue," in Plutarch, *Mor.* 452C). Polycarp already cited Paul's advice here in 110 CE (*Phil.* 11—and as a genuine letter of Paul!). Titus 3:10-11 and Rom 16:17-20 identify the *next* step when a person does not respond to admonitions. Deuteronomy also required evil to be purged from the congregation's midst (Deut 17:7; 19:19; 21:21; 22:24; 24:7; also Matt 18:17-18; 1QS VI, 24—VII, 27; IX, 3-6).[30]

Paul asks that the Lord give peace to them at all times[31] and in every way (v. 16) (also Num 6:26 LXX; Isa 26:12-13 LXX; the "God of peace" in 1 Thess 5:23; Rom 15:33; 16:20; 2 Cor 13:11; Phil 4:7, 9). For Paul, the Lord is the Son, but only here is he "the Lord of peace," a departure from his usual "God of peace" and reflecting the high Christological emphasis of this letter (Yahweh in the OT [Judg 6:12; Ruth 2:4; 2 Chr 15:2]). Behind the Greek word is the Hebrew *shalom*.

On the wish for peace, see also Rom 16:20 (after Paul had just corrected a problem); 2 Cor 13:11; Gal 6:16. The Lord *himself* will have to *give* this peace in the presence of disorderly members of the congregation; unlike "the God of peace *be with* you" elsewhere. This correction is intended not to alienate but to bring peace! "The Lord be with all of you" (even the idlers) is reminiscent of Ruth 2:4 (also Judg 6:12; 2 Chr 15:2; Luke 1:28).[32]

Paul writes in his own hand (v. 17; similarly, 1 Cor 16:21 [Paul's next letter?]; Col 4:18; Cicero, *Att.* 8.1.1; 13.28.4). Paul writes in this way, and thus people are to recognize the handwriting when he takes the letter from the scribe to sign (Gal 6:11 and the recognizable size of Paul's letters; also Phlm 19). Recognition of the prior pattern here indicates that not only 1 Thessalonians *but also Galatians* (as Paul's earliest letter) predated 2 Thessalonians.[33] In emphasizing in this letter teaching that came *directly* from him, Paul may also have been guarding against the possibility of future forgeries in his name. The handwriting would also

---

30. On removing "cancerous" individuals, see Lee, *Paul*, 40-41.

31. "At all times"—see, e.g., Matt 18:10; Mark 5:5; Luke 24:53; Acts 2:25; 10:2; 24:16; Rom 11:10.

32. Fee, *Thessalonians*, 341.

33. Das, *Galatians*, 31-47.

combat false messages claiming to be from him at Thessalonica (2 Thess 2:2, 15) and would convey his personal authority. The grace of the Lord Jesus Christ is to be on *all* the Thessalonians, even the disorderly (v. 18; identical in 1 Thess 5:28). This concluding benediction is also similar to 1 Cor 16:23; Gal 6:18; Phil 4:23; Phlm 25.

Select Bibliography

Ambrose. *Letters.* Translated by Mary Melchior Beyenka. FC 26. New York: Fathers of the Church, 1954.
Ambrosiaster. *Commentaries on Galatians-Philemon.* Edited and translated by Gerald L. Bray. Ancient Christian Texts. Downers Grove, IL: IVP Academic, 2009.
Aquinas, Thomas. *Commentary on Saint Paul's First Letter to the Thessalonians and the Letter to the Philippians.* Translated by F. R. Larcher and Michael J. Duffy. Aquinas Scripture Series 3. Albany, NY: Magi, 1969.
Arminius, James. *The Works of James Arminius.* Translated by James Nichols. 3 vols. Grand Rapids: Baker, 1986.
Athanasius. *The Resurrection Letters.* Edited by Jack N. Sparks. Nashville: Nelson, 1979.
Augustine. *Commentary on the Lord's Sermon on the Mount with Seventeen Related Sermons.* Translated by Denis J. Kavanagh. FC 11. Washington, DC: Catholic University of America Press, 1951.
———. *Letters.* Translated by Wilfrid Parsons. Vol. 4 of *Saint Augustine.* FC 30. Washington, DC: Catholic University of America Press, 1955.
———. *Tractates on the Gospel of John 28–54.* Translated by John W. Rettig. FC 88. Washington, DC: Catholic University of America Press, 1993.
———. *The Works of St. Augustine: A Translation for the 21st Century.* Edited by John E. Rotelle. New York: New City Press, 1990–.
Aus, Roger D. "The Liturgical Background of the Necessity and Propriety of Giving Thanks According to 2 Thess 1.3." *JBL* 92 (1973) 432–38.
Barclay, John M. G. "Conflict in Thessalonica." *CBQ* 55 (1993) 512–30.
———. "Thessalonica and Corinth: Social Contrasts in Pauline Christianity." *JSNT* 15 (1992) 49–74.
Basil of Caesarea. "The Long Rules." In *Saint Basil: Ascetical Works,* translated by M. Monica Wagner, 223–338. FC 9. New York: Fathers of the Church, 1950.
Bassler, Jouette M. "The Enigmatic Sign: 2 Thessalonians 1:5." *CBQ* 46 (1984) 496–510.
Beale, G. K. *1–2 Thessalonians.* IVP New Testament Commentary Series 13. Downers Grove, IL: IVP Academic, 2003.
Bede the Venerable. *Excerpts from the Works of Saint Augustine on the Letters of the Blessed Apostle Paul.* Translated by David Hurst. Kalamazoo, MI: Cistercian, 1999.
Bengel, Johann Albrecht. *Gnomon Novi Testamenti.* Tübingen: Schramm, 1742.
———. *Gnomon of the New Testament.* 2 vols. Philadelphia: Perkinpine & Higgins, 1860.

SELECT BIBLIOGRAPHY

———. *New Testament Word Studies*. Grand Rapids: Kregel, 1971.
Best, Ernest. *A Commentary on the First and Second Epistles to the Thessalonians*. HNTC. New York: Harper & Row, 1972.
Boring, M. Eugene. *I and II Thessalonians: A Commentary*. NTL. Louisville: Westminster John Knox, 2015.
Bounds, E. M. *The Essentials of Prayer*. Rev. ed. Grand Rapids: Baker, 1990. First published 1925.
Brocke, Christoph vom. *Thessaloniki—Stadt des Kasssander und Gemeinde des Paulus: Eine frühe christliche Gemeinde in ihrer heidnischen Umwelt*. WUNT 2/125. Tübingen: Mohr Siebeck, 2001.
Brookins, Timothy A. *First and Second Thessalonians*. Paideia Commentaries on the New Testament. Grand Rapids: Baker, 2021.
Bruce, F. F. *1 and 2 Thessalonians*. WBC 45. Waco, TX: Word, 1982.
Calvin, John. *The Epistles of Paul the Apostle to the Romans and to the Thessalonians*. Translated by Ross Mackenzie. Calvin's Commentaries. Grand Rapids: Eerdmans, 1961.
———. *Institutes of the Christian Religion*. Translated by Henry Beveridge. 1845–46. Repr., Peabody, MA: Hendrickson, 2008.
Carson, D. A., and Douglas J. Moo. *An Introduction to the New Testament*. Grand Rapids: Zondervan, 2005.
Caswall, Edward, trans. "Hark! A Thrilling Voice Is Sounding." Hymnary, [1861]. https://hymnary.org/text/hark_a_thrilling_voice_is_sounding.
Chadwick, H. "1 Thess 3³: σαίνεσθαι." *JTS* 1 (1950) 156–58.
Cicero. *Letters to Atticus*. Translated by Eric Otto Winstedt. 3 vols. LCL. Cambridge, MA: Harvard University Press, 1920–25.
Collins, Adela Yarbro. "Vilification and Self-Definition in the Book of Revelation." *HTR* 79 (1986) 308–20.
Cosby, Michael R. "Hellenistic Formal Receptions and Paul's Use of ΑΠΑΝΤΗΣΙΣ in 1 Thessalonians 4:17." *BBR* 4 (1994) 15–34.
Cyril of Alexandria. *Letters 51–110*. Translated by John I. McEnerney. FC 77. Washington, DC: Catholic University of America Press, 1987.
Das, A. Andrew. *Galatians*. ConC. St. Louis: Concordia, 2014.
———. *Paul and the Jews*. Library of Pauline Studies. Peabody, MA: Hendrickson, 2003.
———. *Remarriage in Early Christianity*. Grand Rapids: Eerdmans, 2024.
Deissmann, Adolf. *Light from the Ancient East*. Grand Rapids: Baker, 1965.
Denney, James. *The Epistles to the Thessalonians*. London: Hodder & Stoughton, 1909.
Donfried, Karl P. "The Cults of Thessalonica and the Thessalonian Correspondence." *NTS* 31 (1985) 336–56.
Edson, Charles. "Cults of Thessalonica: Macedonia III." *HTR* 41 (1948) 153–204.
———. "Macedonia." *Harvard Studies in Classical Philology* 51 (1948) 125–36.
Edwards, Jonathan. "Sinners in the Hands of an Angry God." In *Writings from the Great Awakening*, edited by Philip F. Gura, 625–41. Library of America 245. New York: Library of America, 2013.
Ellicott, Charles John. *Commentary on the Epistles of St. Paul to the Thessalonians*. Grand Rapids: Zondervan, 1957.
Erasmus, Desiderius. "Enchiridion." In *Advocates of Reform: From Wyclif to Erasmus*, edited by Matthew Spinka, 295–379. LCC 14. Philadelphia: Westminster, 1953.

SELECT BIBLIOGRAPHY

Estii, Guiliemi. *In Omnes Divi Pauli Epistolas, item in Catholicas Commentarii.* 3 vols. Mainz: Sumptibus Francisci Kirschhemi, 1858–59. First published 1614–16.

Euripides. *"Alcestis" and Other Plays.* Translated by Philip Vellacott. Penguin Classics. London: Penguin, 1953.

Evans, Robert Maxwell. "Eschatology and Ethics: A Study of Thessalonica and Paul's Letters to the Thessalonians." PhD diss., University of Basel, 1968.

Fee, Gordon D. *The First and Second Letters to the Thessalonians.* NICNT. Grand Rapids: Eerdmans, 2009.

Foster, Paul. "Who Wrote 2 Thessalonians: A Fresh Look at an Old Problem." *JSNT* 35 (2012) 150–75.

Fudge, Edward. "The Final End of the Wicked." *JETS* 27 (1984) 325–34.

Furnish, Victor Paul. *1 Thessalonians, 2 Thessalonians.* ANTC. Nashville: Abingdon, 2007.

Gerber, Christine. *Paulus und seine "Kinder": Studien zur Beziehungsmetaphorik der paulinischen Briefe.* BZNW 136. Berlin: de Gruyter, 2005.

Green, Gene L. *The Letters to the Thessalonians.* Pillar New Testament Commentary. Grand Rapids: Eerdmans, 2002.

Gundry, Robert H. "A Brief Note on 'Hellenistic Formal Receptions and Paul's Use of ΑΠΑΝΤΗΣΙΣ in 1 Thessalonians 4:17.'" *BBR* 6 (1996) 39–41.

———. "The Hellenization of Dominical Tradition and Christianization of Jewish Tradition in the Eschatology of 1–2 Thessalonians." *NTS* 33 (1987) 161–78.

Gupta, Nijay K. *Paul and the Language of Faith.* Grand Rapids: Eerdmans, 2020.

Haimo of Auxere. *Exposition of the Second Letter to the Thessalonians.* In *Second Thessalonians: Two Early Medieval Apocalyptic Commentaries*, translated by Kevin L. Hughes, 13–33. Kalamazoo: Western Michigan University Press, 2001.

Hannah, Darrell D. "The Angelic Restrainer of 2 Thessalonians 2.6–7." In *Calling Time: Religion and Change at the Turn of the Millennium*, edited by Martyn Percy, 28–45. Lincoln Studies in Religion and Society 2. Sheffield: Sheffield Academic, 2000.

———. *Michael and Christ: Michael Traditions and Angel Christology in Early Christianity.* WUNT 2/109. Tübingen: Mohr Siebeck, 1999.

Harrison, James R. *Paul and the Imperial Authorities at Thessalonica and Rome: A Study in the Conflict of Ideology.* WUNT 1/273. Tübingen: Mohr Siebeck, 2011.

Hartman, Lars. "The Eschatology of 2 Thessalonians as Included in a Communication." In *The Thessalonian Correspondence*, edited by Raymond F. Collins, 470–85. BETL 87. Leuven: Leuven University Press, 1990.

Hendrix, Holland L. "Thessalonike." In *Archaeological Resources for New Testament Studies*, edited by Helmut Koester and Holland L. Hendrix, 1:1–49. Philadelphia: Fortress, 1987.

Henry, Matthew. *Concise Commentary on the Whole Bible.* Chicago: Moody, 1981.

Hock, Ronald F. *The Social Context of Paul's Ministry: Tentmaking and Apostleship.* Minneapolis: Fortress, 1980.

———. "The Workshop as a Social Setting for Paul's Missionary Preaching." *CBQ* 41 (1979) 438–50.

Holtz, Traugott. "On the Background of 1 Thessalonians 2:1–12." In *The Thessalonians Debate: Methodological Discord or Methodological Synthesis?*, edited by Karl P. Donfried and Johannes Beutler, 69–80. Grand Rapids: Eerdmans, 2000.

Howard, Tracy L. "The Literary Unity of 1 Thessalonians 4:13—5:11." *Grace Theological Journal* 9 (1988) 163–90.

SELECT BIBLIOGRAPHY

Hurtado, Larry W. *Lord Jesus Christ: Devotion to Jesus in Earliest Christianity.* Grand Rapids: Eerdmans, 2003.

Hus, John. "On Simony." In *Advocates of Reform*, edited by Matthew Spinka, 196–278. LCC 14. Philadelphia: Westminster, 1953.

Jewett, Robert. *The Thessalonian Correspondence: Pauline Rhetoric and Millenarian Piety.* Foundations and Facets. Philadelphia: Fortress, 1986.

Jowett, Benjamin. *The Epistles of St. Paul to the Thessalonians, Galatians, Romans.* 2nd ed. 2 vols. London: Murray, 1859.

Kim, Seyoon. *Paul's Gospel for the Thessalonians and Others: Essays on 1 and 2 Thessalonians and Other Pauline Epistles.* WUNT 1/481. Tübingen: Mohr Siebeck, 2022.

Kim, Seyoon, and F. F. Bruce. *1 and 2 Thessalonians.* 2nd ed. WBC 45. Grand Rapids: Zondervan, 2023.

Koester, Helmut. *Paul and His World: Interpreting the New Testament in Its Context.* Minneapolis: Fortress, 2007.

Lausberg, Heinrich. *Handbuch der literarischen Rhetorik.* 2 vols. 2nd ed. Munich: Hueber, 1973.

Law, William. *A Serious Call to a Devout and Holy Life.* Philadelphia: Westminster, 1948.

Lee, Michelle V. *Paul, the Stoics, and the Body of Christ.* SNTSMS 137. Cambridge: Cambridge University Press, 2006.

Levinskaya, Irina. *Diaspora Setting.* Vol. 5 of *The Book of Acts in Its First Century Setting.* Grand Rapids: Eerdmans, 1996.

Lightfoot, J. B. *Biblical Essays.* 1893. Repr., Peabody, MA: Hendrickson, 1994.

Lünemann, Gottlieb. *Critical and Exegetical Handbook to the Epistles of St. Paul to the Thessalonians.* Edinburgh: T. & T. Clark, 1880.

Luther, Martin. "An Appeal to the Ruling Class." In *Martin Luther: Selections from His Writings*, edited by John Dillenberger, 403–85. Garden City, NY: Doubleday, 1961.

———. "Bondage of the Will." In *Career of the Reformer 3*, edited and translated by Philip S. Watson, 3–295. Vol. 33 of *Luther's Works*. Philadelphia: Fortress, 1972.

———. "Epistle to the Hebrews." In *Luther: Early Theological Works*, edited and translated by James Atkinson, 29–250. LCC 16. Philadelphia: Westminster, 1962.

———. "Freedom of the Christian." In *Career of the Reformer 1*, edited by Harold J. Grimm, 333–77. Vol. 31 of *Luther's Works*. Philadelphia: Muhlenberg, 1957.

———. "Katy Recommended as Teacher of German, Nov. 4, 1538—No. 4081." In *Table Talk*, edited by Theodore G. Tappert, 317–18. Vol. 54 of *Luther's Works*. Philadelphia: Fortress, 1967.

———. "Lectures on 1 Timothy." In *Selected Pauline Epistles*, edited by Hilton C. Oswald, 217–384. Vol. 28 of *Luther's Works*. St. Louis: Concordia, 1973.

———. "Letter 6." In *Luther's Correspondence and Other Contemporary Letters 1*, edited and translated by Preserved Smith, 28–29. Philadelphia: Lutheran Publication Society, 1913.

———. "Letter 248 to Thomas Zink, April 22, 1532." In *Letters 3*, edited by Gottfried G. Krodel, 50–53. Vol. 50 of *Luther's Works*. Philadelphia: Fortress, 1975.

———. *Luther: Letters of Spiritual Counsel.* Edited and translated by Theodore G. Tappert. LCC 18. London: SCM, 1955.

———. "On the Jews and Their Lies." In *Christian in Society 4*, edited by Franklin Sherman, 137–306. Vol. 47 of *Luther's Works*. Philadelphia: Fortress, 1971.

———. "The Pagan Servitude of the Church." In *Martin Luther: Selections from His Writings*, edited by John Dillenberger, 249–359. Garden City, NY: Doubleday, 1961.

———. "Preface to the Burial Hymns to the Christian Reader." In *Liturgy and Hymns*, edited by Ulrich S. Leupold, 325–31. Vol. 53 of *Luther's Works*. Philadelphia: Fortress, 1965.

———. "That Jesus Christ Was Born a Jew." In *Christian in Society 2*, edited by Walther I. Brandt, 199–229. Vol. 45 of *Luther's Works*. Philadelphia: Muhlenberg, 1962.

Malherbe, Abraham J. *The Cynic Epistles*. SBLSBS 12. Missoula, MT: Scholars, 1977.

———. "Exhortation in First Thessalonians." *NovT* 25 (1983) 238–56.

———. "Exhortation in First Thessalonians." In *Paul and the Popular Philosophers*, 49–67. Minneapolis: Fortress, 1989.

———. "'Gentle as a Nurse': The Cynic Background to 1 Thessalonians 2." *NovT* 12 (1970) 203–17.

———. "'Gentle as a Nurse': The Cynic Background to 1 Thessalonians 2." In *Paul and the Popular Philosophers*, 35–48. Minneapolis: Fortress, 1989.

———. *The Letters to the Thessalonians*. AB 32B. New York: Doubleday, 2000.

———. *Moral Exhortation: A Greco-Roman Sourcebook*. Edited by Wayne A. Meeks. LEC. Philadelphia: Westminster, 1986.

Manson, T. W. "The Letters to the Thessalonians." In *Studies in the Gospels and Epistles*, edited by Matthew Black, 259–78. Manchester, UK: Manchester University Press, 1962.

Marshall, I. Howard. *1 and 2 Thessalonians*. NCB. Grand Rapids: Eerdmans, 1983.

Martin, D. Michael *1, 2 Thessalonians*. NAC 33. Nashville: Broadman & Holman, 1995.

Meeks, Wayne A. *The First Urban Christians: The Social World of the Apostle Paul*. 2nd ed. New Haven: Yale University Press, 2003.

Menken, Maarten J. J. *2 Thessalonians*. New Testament Readings. London: Routledge, 1994.

Metzger, Paul. *Katechon: 2 Thess 2,1–12 im Horizon apokalyptische Denkens*. BZNW 135. Berlin: de Gruyter, 2005.

Milligan, George. *St Paul's Epistles to the Thessalonians*. London: Macmillan, 1908.

Milton, John. *Paradise Lost*. Introduced by Philip Pullman. Oxford: Oxford University Press, 2005.

Morgan, Teresa. *Roman Faith and Christian Faith: Pistis and Fides in the Early Roman Empire and Early Churches*. Oxford: Oxford University Press, 2015.

Mount Olympus 360° View. https://themountolympus.com/the-mountain/mount-olympus-360-view/.

Nicholl, Colin L. *From Hope to Despair in Thessalonica: Situating 1 and 2 Thessalonians*. SNTSMS 126. Cambridge: Cambridge University Press, 2004.

Oakes, Peter. "Re-Mapping the Universe: Paul and the Emperor in 1 Thessalonians and Philippians." *JSNT* 27 (2005) 301–22.

Oetinger, Friedrich Christoph. *Biblisches und emblematisches Wörterbuch*. Hildesheim: Olms, 1969.

Olshausen, Hermann. *Biblical Commentary on St. Paul's Epistle to the Galatians, Ephesians, Colossians, and Thessalonians*. Edinburgh: T. & T. Clark, 1851.

Pearson, Birger A. "1 Thessalonians 2:13–16: A Deutero-Pauline Interpolation." *HTR* 64 (1971) 79–94.

Petersen, Norman R. *Rediscovering Paul: Philemon and the Sociology of Paul's Narrative World*. 1985. Repr., Eugene, OR: Wipf & Stock, 2008.

Plevnik, Joseph. "The Destination of the Apostle and of the Faithful: Second Corinthians 4:13b–14 and First Thessalonians 4:14." *CBQ* 62 (2000) 83–95.

———. *Paul and the Parousia: An Exegetical and Theological Investigation*. Peabody, MA: Hendrickson, 1997.

Poole, Matthew. *A Commentary on the Holy Bible*. 3 vols. London: Banner of Truth, 1685.

Porter, Stanley E. *Verbal Aspect in the Greek of the New Testament with Reference to Tense and Mood*. Studies in Biblical Greek 1. New York: Lang, 1989.

Quarles, Charles L. "The 'APO of 2 Thessalonians 1:9 and the Nature of Eternal Punishment." *WTJ* 59 (1997) 201–11.

Richard, Earl J. *First and Second Thessalonians*. SP 11. Collegeville, MN: Liturgical, 1995.

Riesner, Rainer. *Paul's Early Period: Chronology, Mission Strategy, Theology*. Grand Rapids: Eerdmans, 1998.

Rigaux, B. *Les Épitres aux Thessaloniciens*. Études bibliques. Paris: Gabalda, 1956.

———. "Tradition et rédaction dans I Th. V. 1–10." *NTS* 21 (1974–75) 318–40.

Röcker, Fritz W. *Belial und Katechon: Eine Untersuchung zu 2 Thess 2,1–12 und 1 Thess 4,1–13—5,11*. WUNT 2/262. Tübingen: Mohr Siebeck, 2009.

Schmidt, Daryl. "1 Thess 2:13–16: Linguistic Evidence for an Interpolation." *JBL* 102 (1983) 269–79.

Scofield, Cyrus I., ed. *Scofield Reference Bible*. Oxford: Oxford University Press, 1909.

Smith, Jay E. "1 Thessalonians 4:4: Breaking the Impasse." *BBR* 11 (2001) 65–105.

Souter, Alexander. *Pelagius' Expositions of Thirteen Epistles of St. Paul*. Edited by J. Armitage Robinson. Vol. 1. TS 9. Cambridge: Cambridge University Press, 1922.

Still, Todd D. *Conflict at Thessalonica: A Pauline Church and Its Neighbours*. JSNTSup 183. Sheffield: Sheffield Academic, 1999.

Taylor, Jeremy. "Holy Living." In *Selected Writings*, edited by C. H. Sisson, 42–92. Manchester, UK: Fyfield, 1990.

———. "Humility." In *The Rule and Exercises of Holy Living*, 70–73. London: Longman, Brown, Green, and Longmans, 1850.

Tellbe, Mikael. *Paul Between Synagogue and State: Christians, Jews, and Civic Authorities in 1 Thessalonians, Romans, and Philippians*. ConBNT 34. Stockholm: Almqvist & Wiksell, 2001.

Theodore of Mopsuestia. *The Commentaries on the Minor Epistles of Paul*. Translated by Rowan Greer. WGRW 26. Atlanta: Society of Biblical Literature, 2010.

Theodoret of Cyrus. *Commentaries on the Letters of St. Paul*. 2 vols. Translated by Robert Charles Hill. Brookline, MA: Holy Cross Orthodox Press, 2001.

Thietland of Einsiedeln. *Thietland of Einsiedeln on Second Thessalonians*. In *Second Thessalonians: Two Early Medieval Apocalyptic Commentaries*, translated by Steven R. Cartwright, 35–77. Kalamazoo: Western Michigan University Press, 2001.

Thiselton, Anthony C. *1 and 2 Thessalonians Through the Centuries*. Wiley Blackwell Bible Commentaries. Hoboken, NJ: Wiley, 2011.

Tolkien, J. R. R. *The Two Towers*. Boston: Houghton Mifflin, 2002.

Trilling, Wolfgang. *Untersuchungen zum zweiten Thessalonicherbrief*. Leipzig: St. Benno, 1972.

Tyndale, William. *The Obedience of a Christian Man*. Edited by David Daniell. Penguin Classics. London: Penguin, 2000.

Vincent, Thomas. *Fire and Brimstone in Hell, to Burn the Wicked*. London: Calvert, 1670. https://bibleportal.com/sermon/Thomas-Vincent/fire-and-brimstone-in-hell-to-burn-the-wicked.

Wanamaker, Charles A. *The Epistles to the Thessalonians*. NIGTC. Grand Rapids: Eerdmans, 1990.

Ware, James P. *The Final Triumph of God: Jesus, the Eyewitnesses, and the Resurrection of the Body in 1 Corinthians 15*. Grand Rapids: Eerdmans, 2025.

Watson, Thomas. *A Body of Practical Divinity*. Glasgow: Fullarton, 1834.

Weima, Jeffrey A. D. *1–2 Thessalonians*. BECNT. Grand Rapids: Baker Academic, 2014.

———. "'Peace and Security' (1 Thess 5.3): Prophetic Warning on Political Propaganda." *NTS* 58 (2012) 331–59.

Wesley, Charles. "Lo! He Comes with Clouds Descending." Hymnary, 1758. https://hymnary.org/text/lo_he_comes_with_clouds_descending_once.

Wesley, John. *Explanatory Notes upon the New Testament*. London: Wesleyan Methodist, 1754.

White, Joel R. "'Peace' and 'Security' (1 Thess 5.3): Roman Ideology and Greek Aspiration." *NTS* 60 (2014) 499–510.

———. "'Peace and Security' (1 Thessalonians 5:3): Is It Really a Roman Slogan?" *NTS* 59 (2013) 382–95.

Wilder, Terry L. *Pseudonymity, the New Testament, and Deception: An Inquiry into Intention and Reception*. Lanham, MD: University Press of America, 2004.

Witherington, Ben, III. *1 and 2 Thessalonians: A Socio-Rhetorical Commentary*. Grand Rapids: Eerdmans, 2006.

Wyclif, John. "On the Pastoral Office." In *Advocates of Reform*, edited by Matthew Spinka, 32–60. LCC 14. Philadelphia: Westminster, 1953.

www.ingramcontent.com/pod-product-compliance
Lightning Source LLC
Chambersburg PA
CBHW030901170426
43193CB00009BA/705